A Field Guide to the
Dinosaurs of North America

A Field Guide to the Dinosaurs of North America

and Prehistoric Megafauna

Bob Strauss
Illustrations by Sergey Krasovskiy

GUILFORD, CONNECTICUT
HELENA, MONTANA

FALCONGUIDES®

An imprint of Rowman & Littlefield
Falcon, FalconGuides, and Outfit Your Mind are registered trademarks of
Rowman & Littlefield.

Distributed by NATIONAL BOOK NETWORK
Copyright © 2015 Rowman & Littlefield

British Library Cataloguing in Publication Information Available

Library of Congress Cataloging-in-Publication Data
Strauss, Bob, 1961–
  A field guide to the dinosaurs of North America and prehistoric megafauna /
Bob Strauss ; illustrations by Sergey Krasovskiy.
    pages cm. — (Falcon pocket guide)
  Audience: Ages 5–50.
  Includes bibliographical references.
  ISBN 978-1-4930-0925-1 (hardcopy) — ISBN 978-1-4930-1508-5 (ebook) 1.
Dinosaurs—North America. 2. Dinosaurs—North America—Juvenile literature.
3. Dinosaurs—Museums—North America—Directories. I. Title. II. Title:
Dinosaurs of North America and prehistoric megafauna.
  QE861.9.N67S77 2015
  567.9097—dc23
                                                    2015012789

Contents

Before You Head into the Field

Setting the Scene

Let's take a pretend trip back about 65 million to 250 million years ago to the Mesozoic era, when trillions of dinosaurs roamed the expanse of what we now call North America. Not only trillions of dinosaurs, but trillions of each kind of dinosaur: meat-eating tyrannosaurs, feathered raptors, horned, frilled ceratopsians—you name it.

To put the number into perspective: Only about one hundred billion human beings have ever been born, and that's counting back to an arbitrary starting point of fifty thousand years ago. Raise that number by the vast expanse of deep geologic time and you'll get a sense of how impressive the dinosaurs' two-hundred-million-year dominance really was.

Of course, peek in at any given time in North America's past and you'll see that not all dinosaurs were equally represented. Some were naturally more populous than others (during the late Jurassic period, for instance, plant-eating ornithopods like Camptosaurus vastly outnumbered meat-eating theropods like Allosaurus, for the same reason that there are a lot more wildebeests in Africa today than there are big cats—it takes a large population of herbivorous animals to support a smaller population of meat-eating ones).

Take any slice through deep geologic time, in any region of North America, and you'll find a unique ecosystem: sauropods and hadrosaurs munching on different types of vegetation; small, feathered "dino-birds" and weirdly clawed therizinosaurs joined in an intricate ecological competition for prey; dim-witted stegosaurs and ankylosaurs employing their sheer bulk (and their arsenal of spikes and clubs) to dissuade hungry tyrannosaurs like Albertosaurus.

Let's not forget the environmental conditions in which these dinosaurs lived, which may (over and above the possibility of being stepped on or eaten) pose the single biggest obstacle to your dinosaur-watching expedition. Average temperatures on earth millions of years ago were much, much higher than they are today. We're talking a steady ninety-five or one hundred degrees Fahrenheit year-round, with humidity levels comparable to a Finnish sauna. Even Antarctica, during much of the Mesozoic era, was warm and wet, so you can imagine what life was like nearer to the equator. This hot, humid climate had two salutary effects: It promoted the growth of the trees, shrubs, and ferns at the base of the dinosaur food chain, and it allowed some of these ostensibly "cold-blooded" reptiles to lead a more active lifestyle.

Not only was North America much more muggy during the Triassic, Jurassic, and Cretaceous periods, the continent itself, which then was what's called a supercontinent, looked a lot different, so your AAA road maps won't help you here. Until about two hundred million years ago, North America was part of the supercontinent Pangea, which included the future Eurasia to its northeast, and Africa, South America, Antarctica, and Australia to its south. By the start of the Jurassic period, North America and Eurasia (in the form of the supercontinent Laurasia) had started to separate from the bulk of Pangea (the bigger, southern portion henceforth being known as Gondwana). And by the start of the Cretaceous period, fifty million years later, North America itself had begun to drift westward from Eurasia, as the world's spreading continents started to approximate their modern shapes and distributions.

Given its extreme climate, and its tectonic shenanigans vis-à-vis Laurasia and Gondwana, North America itself was a very different place geologically during the Mesozoic era than it is today. For much of this time, a huge portion of the continent was covered by the Western Interior Sea, which accounts for the profusion of marine reptiles that have been discovered in Kansas. This shallow body of water separated the huge western island of Laramidia (the home of "classic" dinosaurs like Apatosaraus and Stegosaurus) from the eastern island of Appalachia, which had its own unique dinosaur ecosystem. It was only three million years ago that the Central American land bridge formed between North America and South America, which would have fateful consequences for the mammalian megafauna of the time, like the Saber-Tooth Tiger.

But all you want is a selfie with an Ankylosaurus. So why should you care about the deep geologic history of North America? For one thing, this history helps explain why practically every dinosaur discovered in North America had a close cousin (or even a member of the same genus) that lived in Eurasia. That's to be expected, given that these continents spent over one hundred million years in happy wedded Laurasian bliss. It also helps to contextualize the fact that the very first dinosaurs evolved in South America about 230 million years ago and gradually spread to the northern reaches of Pangea (which became Laurasia, which became North America and Eurasia) as well as east and south to Africa, South America, and Australia.

In other words, we can thank Pangea for the worldwide distribution of dinosaurs during the Mesozoic era, but we can thank the breakup of this enormous continent for the subsequent extremes of dinosaur diversity.

Which brings us to another crucial bit of background for your dinosaur-watching expedition: dinosaur evolution. The first dinosaurs of southwestern Pangea (i.e., modern South America) evolved from a family of reptiles called *archosaurs*, which also went on to spawn, during the middle Triassic period, the first true pterosaurs (flying reptiles) and crocodiles. (Simultaneously, an unrelated branch of reptiles—the therapsids—were morphing into tiny, skittering mammals.) The first true dinosaurs weren't much to look at by later standards, but these small, two-legged, insatiable reptiles quickly spread across the length and breadth of Pangea, competing all the while with crocodiles, early mammals, and even the archosaurs that had spawned them (not all archosaurs "turned into" dinosaurs, so significant populations persisted until the end of the Triassic period).

As mass extinctions go, the one at the Triassic-Jurassic boundary was a wet firecracker—"only" about a third of marine species disappeared, and terrestrial animals emerged virtually unscathed, except for some large amphibians and, crucially for dinosaurs, the archosaurs. Now the way was cleared for dinosaurs to assert their dominance. Already by the end of the Triassic period, the first dinosaurs had split off into two key families: ornithischians ("bird-hips") and saurischians ("lizard-hips").

Over the course of the Jurassic and Cretaceous periods, ornithischians evolved into plant-eating duckbills, ceratopsians, and sauropods, while saurischians spawned meat-eating tyrannosaurs, raptors, and small, feathered "dino-birds." (Ironically, birds evolved from "lizard-hipped" saurischians and not "bird-hipped" ornithischians!)

These are the dinosaurs you'll meet in this book, along with a smattering of pterosaurs and marine reptiles.

Those are the broad strokes of the story whose details have been the fossilized bread and butter for generations of ambitious paleontologists. When did the first "thyreophorans" (armored, spiked dinosaurs like Ankylosaurus and Stegosaurus) evolve? How did the late Cretaceous apex predator T. Rex and other tyrannosaurs "improve" upon the late Jurassic Allosaurus? Did birds evolve multiple times during the Mesozoic era or only once, and when, exactly, did they accomplish this feat? How in the world is a person supposed to tell the difference between ceratopsians like Triceratops and Styracosaurus on the one hand, and Agujaceratops and Coahuilaceratops on the other? (There are about a dozen horned, frilled dinosaurs in this book, and if you learn anything after reading it, it'll be that these elephant-like plant-eaters came in all shapes and sizes.)

Another of the things you'll learn in this book is that not everything we know about dinosaurs is written in stone. New dinosaurs are constantly being discovered, existing species and genera are constantly being reassessed, and occasionally it turns out that what we thought were two separate dinosaurs were actually one and the same animal (the classic example is the ornately horned and frilled Torosaurus, which is now considered to have been an unusually old Triceratops). Depending on your age, some of the names in this book may cause you to do a double-take: The ancestral horse once known as Eohippus is now referred to as Hyracotherium, for example. And the once-popular Syntarsus has now been renamed Megapnosaurus (Greek for "big dead lizard"). We won't even get into the whole Brontosaurus/Apatosaurus brouhaha; suffice it to say that your kids are happy with Apatosaurus, while you probably still feel nostalgic for the "thunder lizard."

Evolutionarily speaking, dinosaurs were enormously successful, for an enormously long period of time, over enormous swaths of territory. What went wrong? Well, toward the end of the Cretaceous period, there's some evidence that dinosaurs had hit an evolutionary dead end of sorts and were already declining in diversity. The odds are that they would have survived, though, if it weren't for the meteor that hit the Yucatán Peninsula sixty-five million years ago. The resulting explosion, equivalent to millions of Hiroshima A-bombs, raised a cloud of dust that blotted out the sun everywhere around the world for decades.

First the plants died, then the plant-eating dinosaurs died, and then the meat-eating dinosaurs that subsisted on the plant-eating dinosaurs died. When the dust had finally cleared, a new world beckoned the quivering, mouse-size mammals whose modest metabolic requirements had enabled them to survive this epic catastrophe—and whom you, the reader, can count among your distant ancestors.

Preparing for Your Trip

Observing dinosaurs in the wild isn't like camping out in Yosemite or whitewater rafting down some backwoods river—there are real, life-and-death risks involved, to the extent that some elected officials are calling for an end to this practice altogether. (Dinosaur watching has yet to make it onto the libertarian agenda. You may want to consider writing a letter to your local elected official.) A successful expedition requires weeks, and often months, of physical and mental preparation, as well as an outlay of tens or even hundreds of thousands of dollars. Here's what you'll need to do in advance of your trip:

Memorize Your Dinosaurs

It won't do to head out to the Idaho badlands with a vision of *Jurassic Park*'s Dilophosaurus in your head—all fluttery neck-frill and puppy-dog curiosity—especially since the real Dilophosaurus (page 99) weighs half a ton and doesn't deign to signal when it's about to bite you in half. The same principle applies to Tyrannosaurus Rex (page 205), the arms of which aren't limp, vestigial, and useless but capable of crushing you to this predator's chest with a force of four hundred pounds per square inch. And the same goes for the supposedly "gentle" disposition of five-ton plant-eaters like Triceratops (page 199), which could actually be quite irritable and dangerous when in the proximity of predators and sightseers.

Choose Your Equipment Carefully

Remember that extended sequence in Peter Jackson's *King Kong* remake in which the crew of the *Venture* haplessly stumbles from an Apatosaurus stampede to a T. Rex attack to a bottom-of-the-trench encounter with giant, icky, people-eating bugs? Those are exactly the kinds of scenarios you're likely to encounter on your Mesozoic field trip, and you won't have Jack Black around for comic relief. Make sure each piece of your equipment (binoculars, camcorders, hand-operated reel-to-reel 1930s Hollywood cameras) is as durable and water-resistant as money can buy, and bear in mind that conditions in the wild will be unbearably hot and humid, which may violate the terms of your warranty.

Keep Detailed Records

Remember, you're not only dinosaur watching, you're trying to answer important questions that have eluded generations of paleontologists. Did sauropods like Brachiosaurus (page 72) hold their necks at full height or level with the ground? Did the giant pterosaur Quetzalcoatlus (page 179) actually fly or did it stalk its Cretaceous prey like a two-legged theropod? Did Pachycephalosaurus (page 154) males actually butt one another with their heads for the right to mate with females, or is this a fantasy perpetrated by sexually frustrated evolutionary biologists? If you capture the right bit of video footage, at the right time, you'll be an instant pop-media superstar: Imagine the hundreds of millions of views waiting for you on YouTube!

Pack Extra Food

You never know when you're going to get badly lost; you never know when your SUV is going to pop an axle; you never know when a Category 5 hurricane is going to sneak over the Western Interior Sea and plunge the local ecosystem under fifteen feet of water. More to the point, you never know whether that pack of Deinonychus (page 97) is feeling mellow and sated from a recent kill or is preparing to draw the Cretaceous equivalent of straws to decide which one will allow itself to be cannibalized in order to ensure the survival of the pack. A trunkful of Costco steaks can go a long way toward ensuring your party's safety. The good news is that you won't have to keep them on ice. The bad news is that you'll have to endure the stench during the last leg of your trip, and you may attract an unwanted parade of hungry Troodons (page 202).

Keep Distractions to a Minimum

Beginning dinosaur-watchers, especially, dread the lonely prospect of spending two or three weeks away from civilization and may surreptitiously pack their smartphones and tablets in with more necessary items like anti-giant-mosquito spray and electrified fences. Here are a couple of important points to keep in mind: First, it's virtually impossible to recharge a Samsung touch screen in the middle of late Jurassic Montana, and second, the unearthly, moonlike glow of handheld electronic devices will attract all kinds of unwelcome wildlife to your campsite (and by "unwelcome wildlife," I mean feathered theropods like Chirostenotes [page 90] that will pick your carcass clean before your Candy Crush screen has a chance to refresh).

Drill, Drill, Drill

Just as the military personnel on aircraft carriers spend half their waking hours preparing for events that rarely happen—galley fires, twenty-foot tsunamis, snapped arresting wires that send Shadow fighter jets and their pilots tumbling into the sea—so you and your family will benefit from rehearsing worst-possible-case scenarios well in advance of your trip. Classic drills that should figure on your training agenda include "Hungry Raptor Emerging from the Underbrush," "Sauropod Whipping Its Pointy Tail," "Breaching Plesiosaur," and above all else, "Ceratopsian Stampede": If you don't know exactly what to do when that herd of Styracosaurus (page 196) gets spooked by a T. Rex, it'll be up to some teenaged intern from the US Fish and Wildlife Service to wash your bloodstains from the desert sand.

Leave the Kids and Pets at Home

Yes, a trip to late Triassic New Mexico to see the Lost City of Coelophysis (page 95) is the kind of memory your three-year-old will treasure for an entire lifetime. The trouble is, that lifetime won't extend much beyond her irresistible impulse not only to hug a newborn hatchling but to push it off a short ledge and see if it can fly (kids that age aren't exactly well versed in the difference between dinosaurs and pterosaurs). As a general rule, any dogs, cats, or toddlers you take along on your dinosaur-watching trip should be exceptionally well trained, not easily flustered, and (most important) willing to pee and poop in the vicinity of your Humvee if an expedition farther afield is ill-advised.

In most states this isn't a hard-and-fast rule, but common sense should dictate what written regulations do not. Just as you wouldn't go extreme caving without apprising a close family member (for all you know, your spouse might not ask too many hard questions about, or even notice, your extended absence), you shouldn't head into the Jurassic swamplands without disclosing your travel plans and ultimate destination to the authorities. Do not, however, allow this essential bit of bookkeeping to lull you into a false sense of security: There's no guarantee that park rangers will rescue you if you wind up surrounded by a Utahraptor (page 209) pack or retrieve your remains if they're not conveniently piled up in one place. Whatever the outcome, though, at least your family will know you died doing what you love.

Dinosaur Fight!

At cocktail parties dinosaur enthusiasts like to strike a pose of selfless nonchalance: "Hey, I don't care if anything dramatic happens out in the field. All I want is for one of those big guys to rub himself against a gingko tree, or raise his majestic neck into the desert sky at sunset, and I'll be happy." What they're really thinking, though, is "Good god, I'd love to see an Albertosaurus opening a can of whoop-ass on a slow, lazy Triceratops. Do I have the right video equipment to capture that? How much would the Discovery Channel pay for that footage?"

If you're prosperous enough to fund a full-fledged dinosaur-watching expedition, your rapidly approaching-middle-age self has probably been warped not only by repeated viewings of *Jurassic Park* I, II, and III, but by all those TV nature documentaries you watched as a kid—you know, the ones where a pack of starved cheetahs disembowel a wildebeest as quickly as you can open a can of StarKist tuna. But while you may understand (hopefully) that the T. Rex wasn't *really* fighting all those Velociraptors, you may not be aware of the extent to which those old TV "classic" nature shows you watched as a kid were faked, a full generation before the reality-TV era. Do you think the cameras just happened to be running when that eagle swooped down and carried away that lion cub? More likely the producers procured the cub from a bankrupt zoo, catapulted it onto a well-lit patch of Serengeti, and yelled "Action!"

The point is, in the wild, actual, real-life dinosaur fights—or for that matter, any type of interactions between predators and prey—are phenomenally rare (and brief) outbursts of violence punctuating hours, days, or even weeks of tedium. Camp out as long as you want in the Utah flatlands, and while you'll see Centrosaurus (page 84) aplenty (and become intimately familiar with the unique smell and texture of Centrosaurus poop), odds are you won't even catch so much as a glimpse of a T. Rex. The reason is simple: Predators, as a rule, have much smaller populations than prey animals, and they prefer to lurk on the extreme fringes of herds—since being seen prematurely would constitute a decided evolutionary disadvantage.

What's worse than spending ten thousand dollars on an all-frills-included dinosaur expedition and not

witnessing a single dinosaur fight? You're right—actually getting to see that fight, which may well be the last thing you ever see. When an eight-ton T. Rex tussles with a five-ton Triceratops, it's not like two cage fighters going at it in a UFC championship match, where the spectators are safely separated from the combatants by yards of wire mesh. It's a stark battle for survival between two overmuscled and under-brained dinosaurs, either one of which could, at any moment, a) inadvertently step on you, b) inadvertently roll over on you, or c) advertently choose to bite you in half (the Triceratops because it's feeling a bit stressed out and defensive, the T. Rex because it's getting tired and needs the Cretaceous equivalent of an energy bar).

Even if you're lucky enough to witness a dinosaur heavyweight fight, and live to tell the tale, you may be disappointed by the outcome. It's only in movies and nature documentaries that predators invariably win out over prey, especially when the two combatants are fairly equally matched. Nine times out of ten, that Triceratops will feint convincingly with its frill and horns, or lash out forcefully with its not-inconsiderable tail, and the T. Rex will retreat to the adjoining mesa with its massive head tucked between its oversize legs. Occasionally, yes, the T. Rex will deliver a quick, surgical, killing bite to the Triceratops's neck or belly, but your odds of seeing that in the wild are about the same as your surviving a one-on-one encounter with a Utahraptor.

So what are dinosaur fights really like? Well, if we're talking predators and prey, prepare yourself for even more disappointment. The fact is that even apex predators like Allosaurus and T. Rex aren't so foolish as to take on a full-grown sauropod or ceratopsian; the cost in energy is too high, and the outcome, too, is uncertain. Rather, these meat-eaters are far more likely to target sick, elderly, or juvenile members of the herd, which may not sound especially fair to the average UFC fan, but is the way nature tends to operate (the operative phrase is "culling the herd"). In fact, from the perspective of the average Albertosaurus, the ideal situation would be to stumble upon a recently deceased Styracosaurus (killed by predators, felled by disease, it doesn't really matter) and tuck right in for supper.

If you're really itching to see dinosaurs fight, forget about the food chain: Let's talk mating season, where the real entertainment is. The fact is that most of the hot, heavy dinosaur-on-dinosaur action involves not the sex act itself (see below) but the vicious sparring among males beforehand to determine who gets to mate with the ovulating females. That's why Triceratops evolved its three-foot-long horns, Lambeosaurus (page 125) evolved the weird hatchet-shaped crest on top of its head, and Pachycephalosaurus (page 154) evolved its extra-thick skull: to inflict damage, sometimes lethal, sometimes crippling, mostly just extremely painful, on other males of the herd or pack.

Unfortunately, the same caveats apply to watching two Styracosaurus alphas go dino-a-dino as they do to pulling up a bale of hay and viewing a rematch of Allosaurus vs. Stegosaurus ("This time it's personal!"). Just like your bar buddies, when they're eager to mate, male dinosaurs are literally seething with hormone-driven aggression and will think nothing of impaling you on their horns, crests, or claws if you so much as look at them crosswise. And don't think the females are any less dangerous. Mesmerized by the fight, they may inadvertently back up and turn you into Jurassic sushi with a clumsily placed hind foot. (By the way, it's possible that in some dinosaur species the females battled for the right to mate, rather than the males. The general principles remain the same, but one imagines that the ratings were much higher.)

To make a long story short, there's a reason why all the good dinosaur fights are in movies and on TV. If that's the only reason you're considering a dinosaur-watching excursion to Idaho and Montana, be kind to yourself, stay in your man cave, and watch an episode of *Jurassic Fight Club* instead. Your wife won't have to cash in that life-insurance policy, and your kids will get a chance to know their dad— at least until you hatch the cockeyed idea of peeping on a pair of dinosaurs as they have sex (see below).

Dinosaur Sex

Birds (which evolved from dinosaurs) do it; bees (which evolved at the same time as dinosaurs) do it; and, of course, dinosaurs did it too, though exactly how they did is anybody's guess. The fact is that for the quadrillion or so times dinosaurs had sex during the Mesozoic era, not a single fossil has been discovered of, say, a pair of Troodon (page 202) in the act of mating. The idea isn't as absurd as it sounds: One famous central Asian fossil preserves a Velociraptor in the act of attacking a Protoceratops (in the heat of battle, they were both suffocated by a sudden sandstorm), and a forty-seven-million-year-old turtle called Allaeochelys has been captured *in flagrante delicto*—not once, but no fewer than nine times. We don't even have a clue about dinosaur sex organs, since soft tissues (like a T. Rex penis) don't lend themselves well to the fossilization process.

As the old saying goes, though, "absence of evidence is not evidence of absence." Clearly, dinosaurs did have sex, since they managed to rule the earth for over 150 million years. Short of capturing a pair of Triceratops doing the nasty—a feat that has managed to elude generations of devoted dinosaur-watchers equipped with high-def video cameras and iPods blasting late-1970s funk music—all we can do is reason by analogy with modern reptiles and mammals.

When most people think about dinosaur reproduction, they're not much concerned with small, feathered dinosaurs like Velociraptor and Chirostenotes (page 90) or even multiton plant-eaters like Pentaceratops (page 163) and Hadrosaurus (page 116), the former vaguely resembling modern birds of prey and the latter landing in the same general ballpark as elephants and rhinos. Eagles, condors, elephants, and rhinos all manage to have sex. It's not difficult to imagine an eager, three-foot-long dino-bird equipped proportionately or a female Coahuilaceratops going into heat and attracting the attention of a nearby male. So far, so good.

The real trouble comes when we imagine dinosaurs on the extreme end of the size scale: gigantic sauropods like Diplodocus (page 105) and Apatosaurus (page 60), which could weigh fifty to seventy-five tons, and voracious, oversize predators like the nine- or ten-ton T. Rex—as well as medium-size salad-eaters like Ankylosaurus (page 57) and Stegosaurus (page 193), whose spikes, plates, and tail clubs would (one would assume) be every bit as intimidating to the opposite sex as to any hungry theropods lurking in the vicinity.

Let's tackle (figuratively) those seventy-five-ton sauropods first. The extant animal closest in behavior and appearance to these giant leaf-munchers is the giraffe, which only weighs about a ton but has pretty much the same posture and elongated neck. Giraffes have sex very, very quickly—the male approaches the female from behind and then goes back to doing whatever it is giraffes do when they're not having sex. This is probably the way Apatosaurus and Brachiosaurus had sex too—with the added possibility that these sauropods did the deed in lakes and rivers, where the natural buoyancy of water would prevent the female from being crushed.

We're on shakier ground when it comes to thyreophoran ("shield-bearing") dinosaurs like ankylosaurs and stegosaurs—but, as Dr. Ian Malcolm says in *Jurassic Park*, "Life finds a way." The problem is that the various knobs, spikes, plates, and other protrusions on these dinosaurs' backs would seem to render the classic rear-entry position impossible, and it's difficult to imagine a five-ton Euoplocephalus (page 113) having either the imagination or the flexibility

to do it any other way. The same applies, to a lesser degree, to duck-billed dinosaurs like Maiasaura (page 128) and Lambeosaurus (page 125), which lack any potentially lethal body armor but are saddled with large, thick, inflexible tails.

For the answer to this conundrum, let's consult the largest reptiles alive on earth today, crocodiles and alligators (which, not so incidentally, are descended from the same late Triassic archosaurs that spawned the dinosaurs). These animals don't possess sexual organs per se but all-purpose cloacas with which they urinate, defecate, and, yes, copulate—and it's only necessary to touch cloacas for a second or two for the male's sperm to be passed along to the female's egg.

Which brings us back to our original question: Why is it so hard to catch dinosaurs in the act? Well, if the cloacal theory is true (not only for thyreophorans but for all the dinosaurs of the Mesozoic era), then copulation may be so brief and unobtrusive as to pass unremarked by human observers, who are more wedded to concepts like foreplay, endurance, and mutual satisfaction. But it may also be the case that dinosaurs are exceptionally modest creatures.

The subject, needless to say, is one of enduring scientific interest, especially among employees of the US Geological Survey who enjoy reading creatively titled grant applications.

Dinosaur Eggs

Here's a riddle for you: From the middle of the Triassic period to the end of the Cretaceous, dinosaurs laid literally trillions of eggs—perhaps a handful at a time for large sauropods and tyrannosaurs like Diplodocus (page 105) and T. Rex (page 205), and a dozen or two at once for small- to medium-size genera like Troodon (page 202) and Stegosaurus (page 193). These eggs were compact, durable, and encased in calcified shells, and they weren't laid willy-nilly but in carefully prepared (and often carefully tended) clutches.

So why have paleontologists discovered so few preserved dinosaur eggs, to the extent that some of the best-represented dinosaurs in the fossil record (like Euoplocephalus, page 113) might as well have budded asexually, like Jurassic fungi?

The answer is that dinosaur eggs, like those Grade AAA Large chicken eggs in your refrigerator, have only a limited shelf life, despite all the precautions nature takes to increase their longevity. Once it was laid, an unguarded clutch of dinosaur eggs was an all-you-can-eat breakfast buffet for any hungry animal in the immediate vicinity, which would raid the nest at any time of the day or night, even if a watchful (albeit dim-witted) adult was standing by, and even at the risk of its own life. Once the eggs finally hatched, the situation was no better, as the newborn dinos were picked off by circling pterosaurs, gobbled up like pint-size hors d'oeuvres by feathered theropods, and possibly (if they were left along the bank of a river or an exposed coastline) gulped down by crocodiles and marine reptiles.

This, by the way, is the reason dinosaurs (and modern reptiles like turtles and crocodiles) lay so many eggs at the same time. From the unsentimental perspective of evolution, it isn't important for all the eggs to hatch, or for all the hatchlings to survive. All that matters is that at least one or two Maiasaura out of a clutch of twenty live to adulthood and propagate the species. Only relatively advanced mammals like elephants, horses, and humans can afford to invest their resources in single births, as their more sophisticated social structures (and increased intelligence) have endowed their offspring with a better chance of survival.

Getting back to our initial point, though: What about all those dinosaur eggs that "failed to launch," so to speak, washed out to seas and lakes before they had a chance to hatch and buried beneath layers of goopy sediment? You might think these would be the ideal conditions to fossilize an Apatosaurus egg, but you'd be wrong: The fact is that eggshells are relatively porous, since developing embryos need a constant supply of oxygen and an outlet for waste products like carbon dioxide. These microscopic openings inevitably allow the entry of harmful microorganisms, which quickly devour the dinosaur embryo, nascent skeleton and all—at which point the shell crumbles into hundreds of untraceable (and usually unrecoverable) fragments.

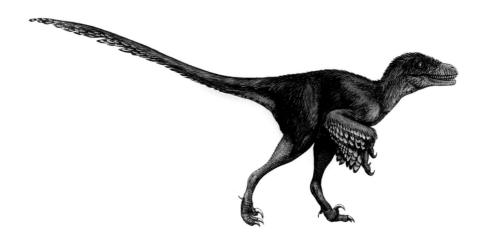

This isn't to say that absolutely no dinosaur eggs have persisted down to the present day—only that they're phenomenally rare, as prized and elusive as the proverbial hen's teeth. If it wasn't for a nearby clutch of fossilized eggs, the central Asian Oviraptor would never have received its name (it turns out that this "egg thief" wasn't raiding a Protoceratops nest but watching, appropriately enough, over its own young). And "Egg Mountain" in Montana has yielded the remains of hundreds of Maiasaura eggs (see page 128), as well as specimens of this duck-billed dinosaur in various growth stages (hatchling, juvenile, subadult, and adult). When they do happen to be discovered, dinosaur eggs are remarkably instructive—but it's nearly impossible to detect intact fossilized embryos beneath their hundred-million-year-old shells, even using state-of-the-art X-ray scanning techniques.

Ironically, even when fossil hunters do happen upon well-preserved eggs, there's no guarantee that the dinosaurs that laid them will be fossilized along with their progeny. What this means is that these eggs are doubly orphaned: The dinosaurs responsible for them have been dead for millions of years, and the embryos inside have been degraded by the ravages of time (and bacteria). The closest we can come to guessing their identity is by shape: The eggs of sauropods, like Apatosaurus, and hadrosaurs, like Maiasaura, tend to be more spherical, while the eggs of meat-eaters like Troodon and Utahraptor are more visibly elongated. (By the way, the largest dinosaur eggs, laid by the largest sauropods, measure a Flinstones-worthy two feet in diameter. There's no denying that that can make a pretty impressive omelet.)

All of the above applies only to dinosaurs. We're on much shakier ground when it comes to eggs laid by other kinds of prehistoric reptiles. Ironically enough, considering the diversity and availability of modern bird eggs, we know next to nothing about the eggs laid by the flying reptiles of the Mesozoic era, the pterosaurs (exemplified by Pteranodon, page 176, and Quetzalcoatlus, page 179)—in fact, the first fossilized pterosaur eggs were only discovered in 2004! And as for marine reptiles like Plotosaurus (page 168) and Shonisaurus (page 184), it's likely that these undersea menaces gave birth to live young while they were swimming—not via a placenta but by the simple expedient of allowing the eggs to hatch while they were still inside the mother's body.

Why have we gone into such excruciating detail about dinosaur eggs? Because there's a particular subculture of dinosaur-watchers—and you may know one yourself— who aren't much interested in tracking a live pack of Coelophysis but can while away an entire afternoon happily humming to themselves as they arrange and rearrange the Anchisaurus eggs on their mantelpiece. Less ethical individuals may attempt to incubate a clutch of Ankylosaurus eggs in their basements and sell the hatchlings on the open market, but these gentler collectors are simply fascinated by the length and breadth of dinosaur egg diversity, collecting and labeling various specimens as if they were Cabbage Patch Dolls or 45-rpm records. If you have no choice but to spend the day with them, you may want to wear unobtrusive earplugs or download an interesting game onto your iPhone.

Dinosaur Packs and Herds

Let's all close our eyes for a moment and try to picture the typical Allosaurus family. There's Dad, slumped in his armchair after a hard day of hunting and scavenging, reading the *Jurassic News* while mom plucks and cleans a five-pound Compsognathus next door in the kitchen. Junior is splayed out on the shag rug, watching *The Flintstones* on TV, while Sis lounges upstairs in her room, chatting on the phone with her BFF about that new, big-frilled exchange student who sat next to her in science class. Meanwhile, the Stegosaurus herd downstairs has put on some loud dance music, and the constant bumping of their plates against the ceiling is eliciting ominous groans from the family's exhausted patriarch, who loudly ruffles his paper, gets up out of his chair, and . . .

OK, that's stretching the facts a bit. As far as we know, no dinosaurs lived in nuclear families (though it's suggestive that some species of birds, which descended from feathered dinosaurs, mate for life and raise their offspring more-or-less together). The more likely Allosaurus scenario is that Dad hit the road after mating with a random female, and mom, after laying a clutch of eggs, pulled the same stunt, leaving most of her defenseless hatchlings to be stomped on by sauropods or gobbled up by smaller predators. It's not as if anyone was in a position to call Child Protective Services 150 million years ago—even if they could get hold of a cell phone, their claws would have been too unwieldy to punch in the numbers.

The fact is that many, if not most, dinosaurs of the Mesozoic era lived an almost completely solitary existence, encountering other members of their species only to: a) battle for the right to mate, b) mate (which may only have taken a few seconds; see page 15), and c) compete for limited resources (one can imagine, for example, two or three Albertosaurus loners converging on a Stegosaurus that died of natural causes, or a group of unrelated sauropods clustered around the same tasty gingko tree). This would help explain why so many dinosaur fossils are discovered in complete isolation—not another representative of the genus within a five- or ten-mile radius—and it also accords with the non-gregarious lifestyles of modern alligators and crocodiles. Life for these dinosaurs was nasty, brutish, short, and above all, lonely.

But not all dinosaurs were doomed to wander, forever bereft, across the plains, woodlands, and valleys of Mesozoic North America. If they were multi-ton sauropods, duckbills, or ceratopsians, the odds are that they lived in herds, aggregations of anywhere from dozens to thousands of individuals. The evidence for this is strongest for Centrosaurus (page 84), a horned, frilled dinosaur whose tangled bones have been recovered by the truckload from quarries in northwest Canada, and for Maiasaura (page 128), which nested in vast communities near Montana's "Egg Mountain." We don't have the same

kind of fossil testimony for huge sauropods like Diplodocus and Apatosaurus, but it seems likely that these plant-eaters behaved like modern elephants, chomping their way through forests and floodplains in groups of a few dozen individuals.

One problem with establishing the herd behavior of dinosaurs is that there can be multiple explanations for why multiple fossil specimens happen to be discovered in the same location. A herd of Styracosaurus crossing a flooded river may all have drowned at the same time, whence their carcasses washed downstream and piled up across a steep incline—but it's also possible that a series of individuals succumbed as they tried to ford the rapids and wound up (thanks to the prevailing currents) in that very same spot, their remains slowly accumulating over weeks, months, or even years. Usually, the hardest-to-dispute evidence of herd behavior is when numerous dinosaurs corresponding to various growth stages—hatchlings, juveniles, subadults, adults, and exceptionally aged "herd elders"— are all unearthed in close proximity.

As for why these dinosaurs traveled in herds, that's an easy question to answer: It's for the same reason that modern sheep, goats, and wildebeest (not to mention many species of birds and fish) stick close together in the wild. Herding is one of nature's premier mechanisms for keeping predators at bay: A hungry wolf or leopard, or even a roaming pack, will be much more hesitant to fight its way through a densely packed herd of prey, and the herd structure allows individuals on the periphery to signal those in the middle that they're in danger (at which point the result is often a stampede). A herd also serves additional social functions. For example, it allows the fittest males and females to easily identify one another and mate, resulting in healthier and better-adapted offspring.

Of course, if you ever watched *Wild Kingdom* as a kid, you know that traveling in a herd is, in itself, no guarantee against getting eaten. That's another consequence of the herding instinct: It allows predators to pick off any individuals who can't keep up with (or who manage to stray away from) the herd, including sick, elderly, and injured adults, as well as newborns and juveniles. A hungry Tyrannosaurus Rex, for example, would be extremely unlikely to attack the alpha male of a Triceratops herd. Rather, it would linger on the fringes and then pounce on any less-imposing trikes lagging or limping behind. (Of more direct interest to dinosaur-watchers, the detection of the T. Rex would likely trigger a stampede, which you don't want to find yourself on the receiving end of.)

We're on much shakier ground when it comes to the evolutionary counterpart of ceratopsian and hadrosaur herds, that is, packs of raptors, tyrannosaurs, and feathered dino-birds. The fact is that it takes a fair amount of brainpower and social cohesion to hunt in packs, and we don't have a whole lot of evidence that dinosaurs measured up to these standards. Any popular misconceptions to the contrary can be traced to the first *Jurassic Park* movie, which convinced an entire generation of impressionable kids that Velociraptors stalked their prey in closely coordinated teams worthy of Navy SEALs (and also advanced the unlikely hypothesis that they were smart enough to turn doorknobs). It's an arresting image, to be sure, but like much else in the movie, it's based on fantasy, not hard fossil evidence.

Still, there is some tantalizing evidence that theropod dinosaurs might—and the operative word here is "might"—have hunted in packs. For that, we have to venture out of the confines of North America to Argentina's Patagonia region, where paleontologists have discovered the remains of the ten-ton, bigger-than-T. Rex Giganotosaurus in close proximity to those of Argentinosaurus, possibly the largest dinosaur that ever lived, measuring over one hundred feet from head to tail and weighing in the neighborhood of one hundred tons. Although there's no way a pack of even three or four Giganotosaurus males could hope to take down a full-grown, one-hundred-ton Argentinosaurus, one imagines that some degree of cooperation would be necessary to hunt and kill a ten-ton juvenile. It's not proof, not by a long shot, but it's a tantalizing hint that at least some dinosaurs were pack hunters.

In the climax of the late, unlamented *Walking with Dinosaurs 3D*, a small pack of Gorgosaurus threatens a migrating herd of Pachyrhinosaurus (page 157). Is this the kind of scene you're likely to see, in real life, on your next dinosaur-watching expedition to Canada's Alberta province? Well, it's possible, but you'll have to be extraordinarily lucky, and you'll have to hope that evolution has endowed Gorgosaurus (a close relative of Albertosaurus and T. Rex) with some significant gray matter. But don't expect to witness anything resembling this movie's big twist, in which a group of tired and hungry Pachyrhinosaurus teenagers, sick of being bullied, turn the tables on their big-toothed tormentors. When it comes to the social behavior of dinosaurs, there are facts, there are reasonable extrapolations from the facts, and there are Hollywood fantasies that even a four-year-old would have a hard time believing.

Know Your Dinosaurs!

Remember those innocent days of toddlerhood, when you were only aware of—and for all intents and purposes, only needed to know about—two or three types of dinosaurs? Stegosaurus, T. Rex, maybe a Triceratops or two—that's all you required to keep you happy, humming, and engaged for hours in the backyard.

Fast-forward thirty or forty years, and there are more dinosaurs than you can shake a proverbial stick at—about one thousand named genera, of which a good three-quarters stand on relatively solid ground, the rest being based on dubious, poorly understood, or nonexistent fossil evidence. How can you possibly hope to keep up without some kind of Mesozoic scorecard?

You can't, short of turning yourself into a living, breathing dinosaur encyclopedia. But you can at least get a head start on the problem by learning about the different types of dinosaurs, the broad families (some widely accepted and well defined, some not so widely accepted and fuzzily defined) to which individual species are assigned. Let's start with the meat-eaters, or theropods, which can be roughly divided as follows:

Early theropods. A few million years after the first dinosaurs evolved in South America, true theropods like Coelophysis (page 95) had spread to North America (230 million years ago, both these landmasses were joined together in the giant continent of Pangea). These early carnivores were slender, scaly-skinned rather than feathered, and may have lived and hunted in extensive packs. It's unlikely that any of them weighed more than one hundred pounds, max.

Late theropods. Entire books have been written about the exquisite, and often obscure, anatomical differences between the two-legged, meat-eating dinosaurs of the Jurassic and Cretaceous periods. "Late theropods" isn't the term a self-respecting paleontologist would use, but it covers a bewildering array of abelisaurs, carnosaurs, allosaurs, spinosaurs, and various other "-saurs" that ranged the gamut from petite to plus-size. Examples in this book include Acrocanthosaurus (page 42) and Allosaurus (page 51).

Raptors. Also known as dromaeosaurs, raptors were small-to medium-size, feathered theropods equipped with single, curving claws on their hind feet (which they used to slash and disembowel prey) and relatively large brains. The most famous raptor of them all, Velociraptor, lived in central Asia, but American varieties described in this book include the bigger-than-average Utahraptor (page 209) and the slightly smaller, but still quite vicious, Deinonychus (page 97), after which the "Velociraptors" in *Jurassic Park* were modeled.

Tyrannosaurs. Probably the most famous dinosaur "type," thanks to the ubiquitous Tyrannosaurus Rex, tyrannosaurs represented the apex of theropod evolution: some of these meat-eating dinosaurs attained weights of eight or nine tons, and they had huge, blunt heads and powerful jaws studded with sharp teeth. Besides T. Rex, tyrannosaurs discussed in this book include Albertosaurus (page 48) and Nanotyrannus (page 139). Like raptors (see above), tyrannosaurs were restricted to North America and Eurasia during the Mesozoic era.

Dino-birds. Yet another term that's shunned by paleontologists, "dino-bird" suffices to describe the innumerable species of small, feathered theropods that roamed the world during the age of dinosaurs. Raptors (see above) can be considered dino-birds, as can therizinosaurs (see below), but this name best applies to otherwise plain-vanilla genera like Chirostenotes (page 90). Although they were well represented in North America, dino-birds were especially common in late Jurassic and early Cretaceous Asia, where they have provided incontrovertible evidence in support of the theory that birds evolved from dinosaurs.

Ornithomimids. Also known as "bird mimic" dinosaurs, ornithomimids were feathered theropods that bore an uncanny resemblance to modern ostriches and emus. Like many modern ratites, ornithomimids were omnivorous, and they may have been the fastest land animals of the Mesozoic era, capable of hitting speeds of up to fifty miles per hour (at least in short bursts). The most famous ornithomimid of them all was, you guessed it, the North American Ornithomimus, described on page 151.

Therizinosaurs. Vaguely reminiscent of big, shaggy ornithomimids—in fact, a handful of controversial fossil specimens appear to straddle the therizinosaur/ornithomimid divide—therizinosaurs were bizarre, slouching, pot-bellied, long-clawed theropods that lurched on two legs and were covered with a coat of feathers worthy of Big Bird. (Even more bizarrely, it seems that therizinosaurs were vegetarians, a very odd diet for a theropod!) For years, these strange dinosaurs were believed to be restricted to Asia, until the discovery of the North American Nothronychus (page 142).

And now for the plant-eating dinosaurs:

Prosauropods. Also known as sauropodomorphs, prosauropods can in many ways be considered the "sister group" to the small theropods described above. Like theropods, they were saurischian ("lizard-hipped") and bipedal, but unlike those early dinosaurs, they were herbivorous (or at least omnivorous) rather than devoted meat-eaters. Late Triassic and early Jurassic prosauropods like Anchisaurus (page 54) were the distant ancestors of the giant sauropods of the late Jurassic period like Diplodocus and Brachiosaurus.

Sauropods. If you piled twenty African elephants on a patch of savanna, you might approximate the shape and mass of one sauropod, the breed of giant dinosaurs that dominated the later Mesozoic era. "Classic" sauropods like Brachiosaurus (page 72) and Apatosaurus (page 60) were thick on the ground of late Jurassic North America. By the early Cretaceous, these gigantic plant-eaters had evolved armor plating and spawned the even more gigantic titanosaurs, which spread to every continent on earth, including Antarctica.

Ornithopods. Yet another family that doesn't quite do justice to the breadth and diversity of genera it contains, ornithopods were two-legged plant-eaters that differed from prosauropods in that they were ornithischian ("bird-hipped") rather than saurischian ("lizard-hipped") dinosaurs. Medium-size ornithopods like Camptosaurus (page 78) coexisted with the giant sauropods described above and were a prime source of food for hungry meat-eaters.

Ornithopods gradually evolved (by way of intermediate genera like Iguanodon) into the duck-billed dinosaurs of the later Cretaceous period.

Hadrosaurs. Better known to the general public as duck-billed dinosaurs (though not all of them were equipped with duck-like bills), hadrosaurs were the wildebeest of the Mesozoic era—slow, dim-witted, two- or three-ton plant-eaters that provided a steady source of food for raptors and tyrannosaurs. Most hadrosaurs congregated in herds, and a few North American genera (including Maiasaura, page 128) have left evidence of advanced child-rearing behavior. Later hadrosaurs, like Parasaurolophus (page 160) and Lambeosaurus (page 125), were notable for their prominent, strangely shaped head crests.

Ceratopsians. If there's any type of dinosaur to which North America can lay a special claim, it's the ceratopsians, the breed of horned, frilled, rhinoceros-like plant-eaters typified by Triceratops (page 199) and Styracosaurus (page 196). In fact, over the last couple of decades, more ceratopsians have been discovered in the United States, Canada, and Mexico than any other type of dinosaur. Dozens of newly described genera include Agujaceratops (page 45) and Coahuilaceratops (page 92), differentiated by their oddly shaped frills and prominent (or not-so-prominent) nose and brow horns.

Stegosaurs. Only one major genus of stegosaur lived in late Jurassic North America, but what a genus it was: Stegosaurus, the weirdly spiked and plated dinosaur that has inspired thousands of tiny plastic figurines. Unlike the case

with the ceratopsians (see above), most of the stegosaur action during the Mesozoic era transpired in Europe and Asia, where these prickly plant-eaters evolved their unique forms of defense against predators. Not a particularly large or diverse dinosaur family, stegosaurs were probably doomed by their relative lack of intelligence—Stegosaurus itself only had a brain the size of a walnut!

Ankylosaurs. These armored dinosaurs can be considered the *reductio ad absurdum* of evolution: Over the course of the Mesozoic era, these squat, four-legged herbivores developed thicker and thicker body armor and larger and more elaborate tail clubs, to the extent that the late Cretaceous Euoplocephalus (page 113) even possessed armored eyelids. Not the brightest dinosaur—perhaps only a notch above its close cousin Stegosaurus—a full-grown Ankylosaurus (page 57) would have been virtually immune to predation, unless an enterprising T. Rex figured out how to flip it over onto its back and dig into its soft belly.

Pachycephalosaurs. They were nature's punch line: a breed of medium-size, two-legged ornithopods that evolved extra-thick, rounded, padded skulls, with which the males presumably battered one another for the right to mate with females (or at the very least, butted the flanks of encroaching theropods). Pachycephalosaurs, the "thick-headed lizards," are represented in this book by the North American Stegoceras (page 190) and the eponymous Pachycephalosaurus (page 154), and you're advised to read these entries closely to learn how *not* to prepare for the human mating process.

After (and Before and Beside) the Dinosaurs

Most of the reptiles discussed in this book—as you may have discerned from the title—are dinosaurs. But the fact is that dinosaurs weren't the first reptiles to rule the planet. That honor belongs to the archosaurs, or "ruling lizards," of the Permian and early Triassic periods; the pelycosaurs, or "bowl lizards," the most famous example of which was Dimetrodon (page 102); and another important branch of reptiles, the therapsids, which went on to spawn plus-size mammals like the Saber-Tooth Tiger (page 187) and the Woolly Mammoth (page 212) tens of millions of years after the dinosaurs went extinct. And throughout the Mesozoic era, dinosaurs coexisted not only with pterosaurs and croco-diles but with various breeds of voracious marine reptiles, including ichthyosaurs, plesiosaurs, and mosasaurs.

At this point you may be asking: What exactly is it that distinguishes dinosaurs from these other, no less impor-tant prehistoric reptiles? To answer this question, we have to journey back to the middle Triassic period, when archosaurs were thick on the ground of what would eventually become South America. This was when these nimble, scaly, two-legged reptiles branched off in three directions: One population evolved into the very first dinosaurs (of which Coelophysis, page 95, was the closest North American descendant), another into the very first, very small pterosaurs (the flying reptiles typified by the much larger Pteranodon, page 176, of North America), and the third into the first true crocodiles.

Confusingly, all of these relatively undifferentiated archosaurs, crocodiles, dinosaurs, and (to a lesser extent) pterosaurs continued to occupy the same prehistoric playing field, making it hard to tell one species from another from the perspective of 230 million years. Suffice it to say that dinosaurs had a telltale posture: Whether they were bipedal or quadrupedal, their legs were "locked" in an upright position, unlike the splayed limbs of contemporary turtles and alligators. (Of course, if you're a paleontologist, there are other, more subtle anatomical features that can be used to distinguish dinosaurs from archosaurs and alligators, such as elongated deltopectoral crests, but you're probably not much interested in hearing about those.)

Let's forget about dinosaurs for the moment and focus on these other representatives of the reptile kingdom. First, though, we'll have to introduce three more terms of art, anapsid, synapsid, and diapsid, which refer to the structure of the reptilian skull. Anapsid reptiles lack any characteristic skull openings behind their eye holes; these comprised some of the earliest known reptiles and today are represented (though not everyone agrees) only by turtles and tortoises. Synapsid reptiles have one extra opening on either side of their heads; this is where we file pelycosaurs like Dimetrodon, as well as the therapsids and (by extension) their mammalian descendants. Finally, members of the huge diapsid family feature two characteristic holes on either side of their skulls; this group includes archosaurs, dinosaurs, pterosaurs, and marine reptiles, as well as modern reptiles like crocodiles and snakes.

Got that? OK, here are quick descriptions of some of the non-dinosaur reptiles you'll encounter in this book:

Pelycosaurs evolved from their primitive reptilian forebears (which themselves had only recently evolved from amphibians) during the late Carboniferous period, and were the dominant terrestrial animals on earth by the start of the ensuing Permian, about three hundred million years ago. Dimetrodon, the pelycosaur most often mistaken for a true dinosaur, was distinguished by its prominent sail, which may have been employed as a temperature regulation device (allowing this cold-blooded reptile to soak up sunlight during the day and dissipate it at night). However, Dimetrodon and its relatives were much smaller than the classic dinosaurs of the Mesozoic era, the largest genera only measuring ten feet from head to tail.

Therapsids evolved from the pelycosaurs of the early Permian period. These synapsid reptiles were characterized by their relatively erect postures (though they didn't stand as ramrod straight as later dinosaurs), and most of them were squat, lizard-skinned, and not very bright, kind of like the ancient equivalent of pigs and cows. Crucially, one branch of therapsids developed warm-blooded metabolisms, cold, wet noses, and primitive fur. These "mammal-like reptiles" went on to spawn the first true mammals of the ensuing Triassic period (which, however, were much smaller in scale; most of the mammals of Mesozoic North America resembled mice and shrews).

Archosaurs, which evolved from an obscure, cattle-like family of reptiles called rauisuchians, benefited from the extinction of all the pelycosaurs and most of the therapsids at the end of the Permian period (the Cretaceous-Tertiary extinction sixty-five million years ago gets all the press, but the Permian-Triassic extinction was much wider in scope, wiping out more than half of the world's species!). It's not quite clear why archosaurs thrived while their fellow reptiles were decimated, but it may have had something to do with the structure of their jaws, their slender bodies, and their bipedal postures. As noted above, it was a population of two-legged archosaurs that spawned the first true dinosaurs.

Pterosaurs, the flying reptiles, evolved from a still-unidentified branch of archosaurs during the late Triassic period. The first pterosaurs appeared around the same time as the first dinosaurs, and were fairly small, sporting oversize heads, long tails, and wingspans of a modest two or three feet. These "rhamphorhynchoid" pterosaurs (don't you love how easy it is to pronounce and spell words from paleontology?) eventually gave way to much larger, more robust "pterodactyloid" pterosaurs, of which the North American Pteranodon (page 176) and Quetzalcoatlus (page 179) are prime examples.

Crocodiles, or "crocodilians" or "crocodylomorphs," have a long and illustrious history and have persisted on earth

pretty much unchanged for the last two hundred million years. You may be surprised to learn, though, that some of the early crocodiles of the Triassic period ran on two legs, and some of them were confirmed vegetarians. No one is quite sure how crocodiles managed to survive the K/T extinction (the meteor impact that killed the dinosaurs sixty-five million years ago) while two other reptile families derived from archosaurs—dinosaurs and pterosaurs— went extinct, but it may have had something to do with the amphibious lifestyle of prehistoric crocs, as well as their slight edge in brainpower. (For a typical prehistoric crocodile of North America, see the profile of Postosuchus on page 170.)

Marine reptiles, of which there are various examples in this book, coexisted with their terrestrial and avian cousins all through the Mesozoic era. In rough chronological order—if you'll allow for overlaps and exceptions—the first important family was the ichthyosaurs, or "fish lizards," which looked uncannily like modern dolphins and bluefin tunas (see Shonisaurus, page 184). Then came the more rugged, more streamlined, and more vicious plesiosaurs and pliosaurs, typified by the truly monstrous Kronosaurus (page 122), and after that the even more rugged, even more streamlined, and even more vicious mosasaurs (for an example of which you can check out Prognathodon on page 173). Like dinosaurs and pterosaurs, marine reptiles went extinct sixty-five million years ago, their quick exit perhaps partially attributable to the evolution of plus-size sharks.

Finally—and perhaps of most interest to the average human reader—we come to the **megafauna mammals** of the Cenozoic era. As stated above, mammals didn't suddenly appear after the dinosaurs went extinct. They were lurking underfoot all along, or hiding up in the branches of trees, biding their time and nurturing their tiny yet relatively advanced brains. By the cusp of the modern era, ten thousand years ago, mammals had long since radiated to their full evolutionary diversity, some awkward genera disappearing into the mists of deep time but others (like Hyracotherium, aka Eohippus, page 119, and the Dire Wolf, page 108) bestowing genetic tokens of their primitive selves on modern horses and dogs. The rest, as they say, is history—or possibly the end of history, as "civilized" humans persist in mindlessly wiping out the world's animal species.

Acrocanthosaurus

Meaning of name: High-spined lizard
Size: 40 feet long and 6–7 tons
When it lived: Early Cretaceous (125 million to 110 million years ago)
Where it lived: Western/southern US
What it ate: Other dinosaurs
Best viewed at: Forth Worth Museum of Science and History (Fort Worth, TX), North Carolina Museum of Natural Sciences (Raleigh)

You can actually spot an Acrocanthosaurus from a mile away: It's the forty-foot-long, seven-ton predator that's just gotten a whiff of your noonday sweat and is plodding in your direction at a steady (if not exactly blazing) clip of five to seven miles per hour.

The most distinctive thing about this dinosaur, aside from its general irritability, is the short ridge along its spine, which isn't nearly as striking as the full-on sail of its African cousin Spinosaurus but comes in handy for signaling sexual availability within the pack. (So if an Acrocanthosaurus is charging you and its ridge is colored bright pink, you may conclude that getting eaten is the lesser of two evils.)

Acrocanthosaurus is one of the few theropods (the vast family of two-legged, meat-eating dinosaurs) whose brain shape and function we know in intimate detail. Its brain wasn't particularly big—picture an especially chunky chicken wing with prominent olfactory lobes—and tilted more toward the crocodile than the bird end of the evolutionary spectrum.

Still, this is all the raw intelligence Acrocanthosaurus needed to pick off its preferred, dim-witted prey, including moderate-size hadrosaurs (duck-billed dinosaurs) like Tenontosaurus and the juveniles of huge sauropods like Sauroposeidon (page 181) and Astrodon. (There's some speculation that a series of preserved footprints in Glen Rose, New York, of all places, memorializes an Acrocanthosaurus pack stalking a herd of unidentified sauropods.)

If you do happen to meet an Acrocanthosaurus in the wild, be sure not to mention (or, this dinosaur's cognitive skills being what they are, show it a picture of) its better-known fellow theropods Allosaurus and Tyrannosaurus Rex. Acrocanthosaurus was once thought to be a close relative of Allosaurus, which lived twenty-five million years earlier, during the late Jurassic period, and was, if anything, even less bright—and it's often compared unfavorably to T. Rex, which lived almost fifty million years after and was of roughly the same size (give or take a ton) and disposition. In fact, the dinosaur to which Acrocanthosaurus is most closely related is the equally fearsome Carcharodontosaurus, the "great white shark lizard" of northern Africa, whose remote geographic location means we can't include it in this book.

Agujaceratops

Meaning of name: Aguja horned face
Size: 15 feet long and 2 tons
When it lived: Late Cretaceous (77 million years ago)
Where it lived: Southern US/northern Mexico
What it ate: Plants
Best viewed at: New Mexico Museum of Natural History and Science, Albuquerque (where it may still be called Chasmosaurus)

There's nothing a dinosaur—even one as unintelligent as Agujaceratops—dislikes more than being mistaken for a famous relative. When hundreds of this plant-eater's bones were excavated from Big Bend National Park in Texas a couple of years before the Second World War began, they were classified as belonging to Chasmosaurus (page 87), which lived all the way up in Canada.

The discovery of a complete skull in 1993 finally revealed to paleontologists that they were dealing with an entirely new genus of ceratopsian (horned, frilled dinosaur), and a few years later the genus Agujaceratops was erected. (Why were so many Agujaceratops bones piled up on top of one another? The most likely explanation is that a sizable herd drowned in a flash flood, a not-uncommon occurrence in late Cretaceous North America.)

As any seasoned dinosaur-watcher knows, it can be extremely difficult to distinguish one ceratopsian from the next: Some of these dinosaurs have slightly bigger or smaller horns, some have slightly more elaborate or plainer frills, and even the growth stages tend to differ from one genus to the next (meaning a juvenile Agujaceratops might look very much like a juvenile Centrosaurus, until *bang!* adolescence hits and it's like a bighorn sheep standing next

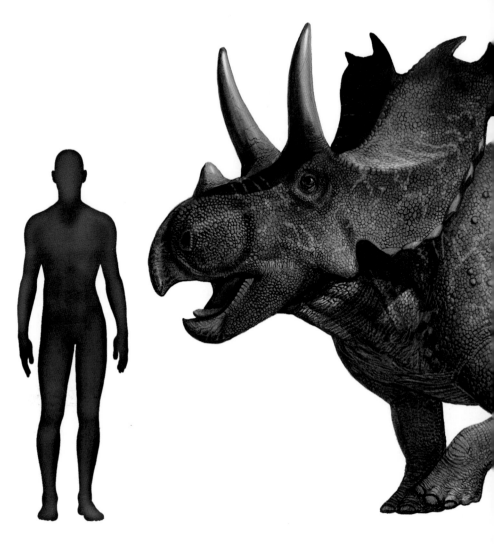

to a dama gazelle). Specifically, the frill of Agujaceratops has a distinctive curve, and its nasal horn is much more prominent than that of its Canadian cousin. As to why these distinctive features evolved in the first place, it likely had to do with intraspecies recognition—if an Agujaceratops got separated from the herd, it needed to find its way back as expeditiously as possible.

While the average Agujaceratops would be proud to have its individuality recognized—heck, it might even agree to pose for you while you take a snapshot—the fact is that the recent discovery of this genus in the Lone Star State opened a veritable floodgate of new ceratopsians: Kosmoceratops, Medusaceratops (page 131), Coahuilaceratops (page 92), the list goes on and on. And new genera are being unearthed practically every week.

While none of these dinosaurs can hope to be as famous as the most notorious ceratopsian of them all, Triceratops (page 199), any one of them, but for a twist of fate, might have been the marquee horned, frilled dinosaur of late Cretaceous North America!

Albertosaurus

Meaning of name: Alberta lizard
Size: 30 feet long and 3 tons
When it lived: Late Cretaceous (70 million years ago)
Where it lived: Western US and Canada
What it ate: Other dinosaurs
Best viewed at: Royal Tyrell Museum of Paleontology (Drumheller, Canada)

Imagine this scenario: You're out in the wilds of northern Canada, leaning comfortably against the trunk of a

blooming conifer tree and leisurely scanning the Cretaceous horizon with your Zeiss Victory binoculars. Suddenly, you notice a juvenile Albertosaurus—no more than ten feet from head to tail and three hundred or so pounds—running full-speed in your direction, which you at first think is cute but then start to take very seriously as there's no indication that the dino intends to slow down.

Putting personal survival ahead of brag-to-your-buddies valor, you grab your gear and start sprinting in the opposite direction. You're about to clear the top of a nearby

hill when a full-grown Albertosaurus appears and lowers its massive snout in your direction. And then this macabre daydream ends, because you've just been eaten.

Is there any proof that Albertosaurus hunted in packs? Well, we may never know for sure, since no field expeditions to Canada's Alberta province have made it back to civilization alive (and their journals and video cameras all wind up mysteriously smashed, as if by an endless stampede of two-foot-wide theropod feet).

Paleontologists have discovered the clustered remains of over twenty-five Albertosaurus individuals, of all ages, in Canada's Dry Island bone bed, but the possibility remains that these dinosaurs clustered together in the wake of some environmental catastrophe (most likely a flood) and not to ally their small brains in the crafty pursuit of some lumbering sauropod.

Does Albertosaurus sound truly terrifying? Are you tempted to take up a less dangerous hobby than dinosaur-spotting, something like lepidoptery or macramé? Well, bear in mind that this carnivore was less than half the size of Tyrannosaurus Rex (page 205), which lived a bit farther east, and was actually in the midsize range as tyrannosaurs go (we won't even mention huge, meat-eating dinosaurs like the South American Giganotosaurus and the African Spinosaurus, which lie outside the scope of this book). If you can't face up to the likes of the Alberta lizard, you might as well trade in your radar-tracking equipment and tranquilizer darts for some sugarless lemonade and go have a nice lie-down.

Allosaurus

Meaning of name: Different lizard
Size: 30 feet long and 3 tons
When it lived: Late Jurassic (150 million years ago)
Where it lived: Western US
What it ate: Other dinosaurs
Best viewed at: American Museum of Natural History (New York), Carnegie Museum of Natural History (Pittsburgh, PA)

Pound-for-pound, and quivering, disemboweled victim for quivering, disemboweled victim, you can make the case that Allosaurus was a far more dangerous dinosaur than Tyrannosaurus Rex (which lived eighty-five million years later and is described on page 205). Allosaurus is even more aesthetically pleasing than its more famous cousin. As you approach it in the wild, you'll have cause to admire its modestly proportioned head and snout, its reasonably long arms (at least compared to the comically foreshortened front limbs of T. Rex), and its overall svelte build, three tons of muscle and bone packed into a slender frame measuring thirty feet from head to tail.

The dinosaur so nice they named it not only twice but four or five times, Allosaurus is famous for having been a cause for contention in the notorious "Bone Wars," the late nineteenth-century feud between the famous American paleontologists Othniel C. Marsh and Edward Drinker Cope. So many Allosaurus fossils were unearthed in Colorado quarries that the result was a profusion of spurious Allosaurus species and Allosaurus-like genera, including Creosaurus and Labrosaurus (named by Marsh) and Epanterias (named by Cope). Further complicating matters, one famous Allosaurus specimen was dubbed Antrodemus; in fact, the name *Allosaurus* didn't come into wide usage until the mid-1970s.

Since there's still a lot we don't know about the hunting preferences of Allosaurus (does this dinosaur pursue its prey in coordinated packs, or are its adults mean-spirited and solitary?), it should be observed in the wild with an abundance of caution. You certainly don't want to get upwind of this meat-eater (especially if you haven't had the chance to shower recently), and soft-soled sneakers are recommended rather than clunky hiking boots, as it may have an acute sense of hearing. If everything goes pear-shaped,

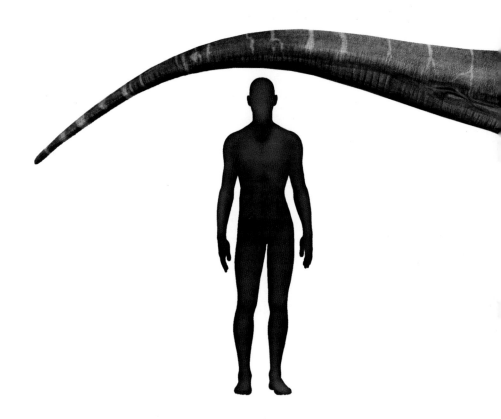

a well-armored SUV should keep you safe for at least a few minutes, assuming you close all the windows, lock the doors, and promptly curl up into a motionless butt-ball in the back seat.

Anchisaurus

Meaning of name: Almost lizard
Size: 6 feet long and 75 pounds
When it lived: Early Jurassic (200 million to 190 million years ago)
Where it lived: Eastern US
What it ate: Plants
Best viewed at: Yale Peabody Museum of Natural History (New Haven, CT)

One doesn't normally associate the state of Connecticut with dinosaurs. Utah, yes. Colorado, yes. But Connecticut is better known for posh educational institutions like Choate and Yale, and affluent burgs like Darien and New Canaan, than for its Mesozoic wildlife. It's the exception to the general rule that no state without a decent barbecue joint can have a cool dinosaur lurking millions of years back in its lineage. (It should be noted, however, that Connecticut is home to some of the best-preserved dinosaur footprints in the world, though apparently housing costs were so high that the dinosaurs themselves didn't bother to stick around.)

Granted, Anchisaurus is nothing like the tyrannosaurs and raptors you're likely to encounter farther out west on your dinosaur-watching expedition. This is a slender, gentle plant-eater, about the size of a healthy sixth grader but (and hopefully, depending on whom you're comparing it to) much less intelligent.

The "almost lizard" is a prime example of what some paleontologists call a sauropodomorph and others call a prosauropod: an ancient side-branch of the line of dinosaurs that went on to spawn the giant sauropods and titanosaurs of the Jurassic and Cretaceous periods. Amazingly, only a few tens of millions of years separate the

seventy-five-pound Anchisaurus from multiton behemoths like Apatosaurus (page 60) and Sauroposeidon (page 181).

Unlike many of the other dinosaurs in this book, there's no chance of an Anchisaurus biting your head off. The most antisocial thing it's likely to do is steal the salad from your picnic blanket and then beg for seconds—and if you approach it too clumsily, this dinosaur is likely to run off on two legs, a comical sight given Anchisaurus's long neck, paunchy stomach, and accustomed quadrupedal posture. (Don't be overconfident, though. Some paleontologists speculate that Anchisaurus and other prosauropods like it occasionally supplemented their plant diets with servings of meat. You'll probably be safe, but you may want to keep your miniature schnauzer in the car just in case. . . .)

Ankylosaurus

Meaning of name: Fused lizard
Size: 20 feet long and 3 tons
When it lived: Late Cretaceous (70 million to 65 million years ago)
Where it lived: Western US
What it ate: Plants
Best viewed at: Museum of the Rockies (Bozeman, MT), American Museum of Natural History (New York)

The first thing a neophyte dinosaur-watcher should say when she encounters a full-grown Ankylosaurus is something like, "Isn't nature wonderful? How provident of evolution to equip this plant-eater with such spectacular armor plating, as a means of defense against hungry tyrannosaurs." What she's more likely to blurt out, though: "Is this thing even alive?" That's because the Ankylosaurus saw her coming from five hundred feet away, flopped down onto its belly, tucked in its head, legs, and tail, and is now doing its best to impersonate a Cretaceous fire hydrant.

Heck, you could probably throw a Sweet Sixteen party on this armored dinosaur's back, and it'll lie there patiently until the iPod dock runs out of charge and everyone goes home.

Of course, this scenario applies only if our hypothetical sightseer approaches the Ankylosaurus all by herself, equipped with a pair of binoculars, a backpack, and a canteen. If she blunders into this dinosaur's domain driving a tricked-out SUV, horns blaring and Lil Wayne blasting on Pandora, she might find herself on the receiving end of Ankylosaurus's massive clubbed tail, which will make a great story to tell her auto-shop technician and the gals in

the book club but may also result in some serious internal injuries. In the worst case, the besieged titan may actually attempt to sit on her vehicle. There's no good outcome here.

Seriously, though, the amazing thing about Ankylosaurus (and other armored dinosaurs like it, which are known, unsurprisingly, as ankylosaurs) is that this was one of the last dinosaurs standing before the K/T extinction. Even though it was built like a Sherman tank and would barely have noticed if a tree fell on it, Ankylosaurus succumbed, just like its cousins, to the frigid temperatures and dwindling food supplies in the wake of that disastrous meteor impact sixty-five million years ago. (Granted, given its cold-blooded metabolism and tiny brain, this couldn't

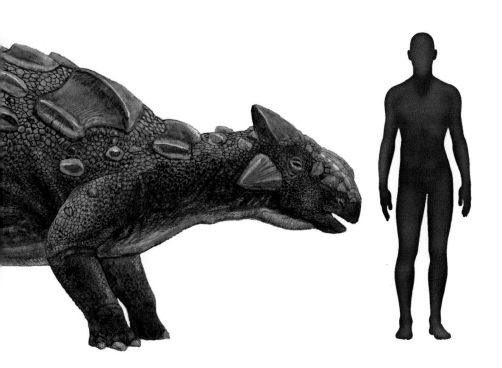

have been the smartest dinosaur that ever lived, so it probably wouldn't have occurred to Ankylosaurus to simply
crawl into that nearby cozy cave and wait until conditions
improved.)

Apatosaurus

Meaning of name: Deceptive lizard
Size: 50–70 feet long and 25–40 tons
When it lived: Late Jurassic (150 million years ago)
Where it lived: Western US
What it ate: Plants
Best viewed at: American Museum of Natural History (New York), Carnegie Museum of Natural History (Pittsburgh, PA)

Getting a close look at a full-grown Apatosaurus requires some solid math skills. Let's say there's a seventy-foot-long specimen idly munching on some tasty cycads about one hundred feet away. How close can you approach before this huge dinosaur senses your presence, pivots around

its ponderous center of gravity, and flicks at you with its twenty-foot-long tail? Take pi to three decimal places, divide by the circumference, carry the four . . . before you know it you've woken up in a field hospital with a whopping headache and a seriously dislocated shoulder ("dislocated," in this sense, meaning it's lodged in a ginkgo tree some three miles to the southwest).

The dinosaur formerly known as Brontosaurus, Apatosaurus is a typical sauropod, the line of gigantic, plant-munching quadrupeds bigger than the house you grew up in. (The story behind the name change is straightforward enough: Apatosaurus was discovered first—by Othniel C. Marsh—and so has precedence over the "Brontosaurus" this same paleontologist described a couple of years later.)

To be fair, we don't know for sure that Apatosaurus cracked its tail like a whip when threatened by predators, but the lack of diagnostic tail marks in the same sediments yielding Apatosaurus footprints is an important clue: This dinosaur clearly held its tail upright, either to defend itself, to keep its balance, or possibly for some other reason.

Tantalizingly, there have been a few scattered sightings of Apatosaurus hatchlings, which seasoned dinosaur-watchers describe as "just about the cutest thing next to a sleeping baby Ankylosaurus." As gigantic as this dinosaur was, its young still needed to hatch from fairly small eggs, and we know for a fact (those preserved track marks again!) that these hatchlings scurried on their two hind legs in order to outrun hungry predators and keep pace with the thundering herd. At what point in their life cycles these Apatosaurus babies finally got down on all fours remains a mystery. If you happen to see this important transition in the wild, file a report immediately with your local paleontology way station.

Appalachiosaurus

Meaning of name: Appalachia lizard
Size: 25 feet long and 2 tons
When it lived: Late Cretaceous (75 million years ago)
Where it lived: Southeastern US
What it ate: Other dinosaurs
Best viewed at: McWane Science Center (Birmingham, AL), Tellus Science Museum (Cartersville, GA)

Rather than describe Appalachiosaurus in boring detail, let's simply review the transcript of a phone call from Tuscaloosa, Alabama, homemaker Beverly Jenkins to her husband, Bill, at work.

Beverly: "Bill! There's something outside the window. I think it's a dinosaur!"

Bill: "A dinosaur? In Tuscaloosa? Are you sure it isn't a hedgehog or something?"

Beverly: "It's much too big to be a hedgehog. For god's sake, it just ripped off one of the gutters!"

Bill: "Dinosaurs live farther west, in places like Utah and Montana. It can't be a dinosaur. Tell me what it looks like."

Beverly: "That's easy. It's peeking in the window right now. Huge snout. Lots of teeth. Beady little eyes. Bill, I think it's a tyrannosaur!"

Bill: (unintelligible)

Beverly: "What?"

Bill: (shouting now) "I said, it can't be a tyrannosaur! Some kind of dinosaur, just maybe, but not a tyrannosaur. Everybody knows tyrannosaurs don't live in . . ."

That's where the transcript breaks off. They found Beverly's torso a couple hours later. You may have read about it in the news.

Anyway, long story short: Yes, there are (or were) tyrannosaurs in the Bible Belt, and they were every bit as imposing as farther-west specimens like T. Rex (page 205) or Albertosaurus (page 48). During the late Cretaceous period, seventy-five million years ago, much of the present-day United States was covered by a shallow body of water known as the Western Interior Sea. Most famous dinosaurs hail from the huge island of Laramidia, on the western border of this sea, but a few have been discovered on the equally huge eastern island of Appalachia, which shares its name with the Appalachian Mountains. That's where Appalachiosaurus comes in. The most complete theropod fossil ever discovered in the eastern United States, this tyrannosaur was the scourge of right-coast-dwelling hadrosaurs and ornithopods.

If you happen to come across an Appalachiosaurus in the wild, don't do what Beverly Jenkins did. Take a picture if you must, then climb into your Humvee and drive away as fast as you can. Appalachiosaurus is more agile than most tyrannosaurs—it only weighs about two tons soaking wet—and its inferiority complex vis-à-vis the hipper island of Laramidia has rendered it especially deadly.

Bambiraptor

Meaning of name: Bambi thief
Size: 4 feet long and 10 pounds
When it lived: Late Cretaceous (72 million years ago)
Where it lived: Western US
What it ate: Small animals
Best viewed at: American Museum of Natural History (New York)

Intensive-care units across the state of Montana are filled with patients who seriously misunderstand the nature of Bambiraptor. Bambi, the Disney character, is an adorable, four-foot-long, doe-eyed, well, doe, who likes nothing better than to cavort in meadows with his pals Thumper and Flower. Bambiraptor, the dinosaur, is a vicious, feathered, four-foot-long sociopath who likes nothing better than to gouge the eyes out of unsuspecting victims using the huge claws on its hind feet. You can see where the confusion might arise, given the similarity of their names, but a few weeks of intensive physical therapy have a way of driving home the difference.

Bambiraptor was famously discovered in 1993, in Montana, by a fourteen-year-old amateur fossil hunter, who stumbled across one of the world's most complete raptor skeletons while on vacation with his family. No less an authority than John Ostrom—the paleontologist who, decades before it was fashionable, theorized that birds evolved from feathered dinosaurs—was called in for an expert consultation.

Soon enough, Bambiraptor was being trumpeted by the world media, even though the suspicion persists in some quarters that it was really a juvenile specimen of another, less ingratiatingly named dino-bird, Saurornitholestes. (At

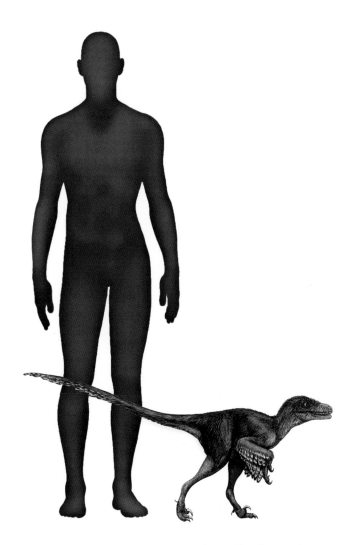

first, some paleontologists even classified Bambiraptor as a species of the most famous raptor of them all, Velociraptor, which lived in central Asia.)

Given that it's more murderous than cuddly, how should you approach a Bambiraptor in the wild?

The recommended technique is to stuff a few dozen gerbils into your pockets, then toss them in this dinosaur's general vicinity (you might want to pack your field trebuchet) and let the feathered menace get its fill. The sated, sleepy Bambiraptor may then consent to a quick pat on the head (be sure to wear your falconry glove!), and it will probably follow you at a cautious distance for the rest of your expedition, eager for more snacks. If you don't provide them, it will hunt you down in a pack and eat you (or one of your children), so be sure to pack plenty of gerbils.

Bistahieversor

Meaning of name: Destroyer of adobe formations
Size: 30 feet long and 2 tons
When it lived: Late Cretaceous (75 million years ago)
Where it lived: Southwestern US
What it ate: Other dinosaurs
Best viewed at: New Mexico Museum of Natural History and Science (Albuquerque)

When dinner table conversation turns to tyrannosaurs, everyone likes to name-drop Tyrannosaurus Rex (or if they happen to live in Canada, Albertosaurus). But the fact is that T. Rex relatives have been discovered all over the United States, ranging from Alabama (see Appalachiosaurus, page 63) to New Mexico, where the oddly named Bistahieversor sails its tyrannosaur flag.

When Bistahieversor's scattered bones were first unearthed in the early 1990s, they were classified as belonging to two other tyrannosaur genera, Aublysodon (from Montana) and Daspletosaurus (from Canada's Alberta province), and this dinosaur was later determined to be close kin to another new tyrannosaur on the block, Lythronax (aka the "Gore King") from Utah.

What led scientists to conclude that Bistahieversor deserves its own genus? For one thing, the jaws of this meat-eater were studded with no fewer than sixty-four razor-sharp teeth, ten more than its famous cousin T. Rex. For another thing, Bistahieversor possessed some strange anatomical quirks, all of which can be explained by evolution but which will no doubt be seized on by conspiracy theorists as evidence that ancient aliens tampered with dinosaur DNA.

Oddly enough, for example, the skull of Bistahieversor has a pair of extra openings above the eyes, and this dinosaur also possessed an unusually long and deep snout (no doubt to accommodate all those extra teeth). The logical conclusion? Bistahieversor was cut off by the Rocky Mountains from the mainstream of tyrannosaur evolution, and so developed in its own unique way.

All that said, what should you do if you happen to encounter a Bistahieversor on the dry, dusty New Mexico plains?

Well, given that you're on said flatlands, this two-ton tyrannosaur will have a clean line of sight and smell and will start rumbling in your direction like a Cretaceous car

carrier. If there are any saguaros nearby, you may want to try hiding behind one, or even jettisoning your gear and scrambling to the top (though it'll have to be a pretty tall cactus for you to evade the clutches of this thirty-foot-long meat-eater, and you'll get stuck by a few hundred nettles along the way, which may make instant death the more desirable option).

Brachiosaurus

Meaning of name: Arm lizard
Size: 85 feet long and 30–40 tons
When it lived: Late Jurassic (150 million years ago)
Where it lived: Western US
What it ate: Trees
Best viewed at: Field Museum of Natural History (Chicago)

There are two—OK, maybe three—kinds of sauropods, the enormous, four-legged dinosaurs that munched their way through the thick vegetation of the Jurassic and Cretaceous periods. The ones most people are familiar with are the "diplodocid" sauropods, whose necks are roughly the same lengths as their tails and who have four equally sized, elephant-like legs and feet (examples include Diplodocus, page 105, and Apatosaurus, page 60).

The second type are the "brachiosaurid" sauropods, with heavily muscled shoulders and front legs that are much longer than their hind legs. The third, "almost" type of sauropod are the titanosaurs, which mostly look like diplodocids but also sport light armor plating.

As you may have guessed, Brachiosaurus is the prototypical "brachiosaurid" sauropod. With its long neck and unequally sized legs, this dinosaur looks uncannily like a giraffe on steroids (in fact, a close relative of Brachiosaurus bears the genus name *Giraffatitan*), and it indulges in some very giraffe-like behavior too, spending its day nibbling the leaves off the high branches of trees.

In the past some paleontologists speculated that Brachiosaurus reared up occasionally on its hind legs, either to reach particularly tasty vegetation or to scare off predators—but the current weight of opinion is that this would cause the sauropod to topple backwards with an enormous thud, knocking itself unconscious and flattening any unfortunate animals that happen to be nearby.

If you happen to spot a Brachiosaurus in the wild, pay close attention to how this dinosaur holds its neck. There have been reports of Brachiosaurus adults stretching their

necks parallel to the ground, like the hoses of enormous canister vacuum cleaners, and inhaling all the ferns and bushes in a fifty-foot radius. However, other dinosaur spotters insist that they've seen full-grown Brachiosaurus holding their necks upright, elevating this dinosaur's tiny-brained head a full fifty or sixty feet above ground level and placing enormous demands on its heart. If this conundrum is ever solved, it will shed much-needed light on the physiology of sauropods, which may be warm-blooded, cold-blooded, or "homeothermic" (that is, they warm up and cool down so gradually that they're able to maintain a near-constant body temperature).

Camarasaurus

Meaning of name: Chambered lizard
Size: 50 feet long and 20 tons
When it lived: Late Jurassic (150 million years ago)
Where it lived: Western US
What it ate: Plants
Best viewed at: Dinosaur National Monument (Jensen, UT), Royal Tyrrell Museum of Paleontology (Drumheller, Canada)

Even though it measures fifty feet from head to tail and weighs in the vicinity of twenty tons (about as much as a fully loaded car carrier or seven bull elephants stacked atop one another), Camarasaurus can be a very hard dinosaur to spot in the wild. Why? Well, this big plant-eater is often obscured by the even bigger sauropods of its North American ecosystem—if there's a seventy-foot-long, fifty-ton Apatosaurus (page 60) standing in front of you, the last thing you're gonna notice is the shrimpy Camarasaurus parked behind its left flank.

Fortunately, Camarasaurus makes up in numbers what it lacks in visibility. This, and not better-known breeds like Diplodocus (page 105) and Brachiosaurus (page 72), was the most populous sauropod of Jurassic North America, at least if you go by the fossil evidence. In fact, it's not inconceivable that Camarasaurus trekked the western plains in elephant-size herds of a dozen (or more) individuals, which would have helped to deter ravenous meat-eaters like Allosaurus (page 51). (Paleontologists have discovered a Camarasaurus pelvis bearing Allosaurus bite marks, a scenario that's almost too painful to think about, especially if you're a leaf-browsing quadruped.)

One common mistake made by novice dinosaur-watchers is to underestimate the sheer bulk of Camarasaurus, since it looks so puny beside its more famous cousins. If you venture too close for a Jurassic selfie, this sauropod

may attempt to shoo you away with a flick of its massive tail, and if that doesn't work, a well-placed stomp of its tree-trunk-like leg will promptly deliver you to Flat Stanley's zip code. Also, the last thing you want to do is set off a Camarasaurus stampede, which will pulverize not only you, the remainder of your party, and your SUV, but any small towns within a five-mile radius.

Camptosaurus

Meaning of name: Flexible lizard
Size: 20 feet long and 1 ton
When it lived: Late Jurassic (150 million years ago)
Where it lived: Western US
What it ate: Plants
Best viewed at: American Museum of Natural History (New York)

Of all the dinosaurs in the Mesozoic bestiary, ornithopods get the least respect. These ungainly, none-too-bright plant-eaters lack the awe-inspiring heft of sauropods and titanosaurs, the prominent horns and frills of ceratopsians, and even the bright-colored head crests of duckbills (into which ornithopods evolved during the course of the Cretaceous period).

In fact, the only reason ornithopods seem to exist is to provide a reliable source of food for large theropods like Allosaurus (page 51), much as the hapless wildebeest today is known far and wide as the "Box Lunch of the Serengeti." In short, there's a good reason so few dinosaur figurines are of ornithopods, even though there are literally dozens of genera, ranging from A (the Asian Agilisaurus) to Z (the Romanian Zalmoxes).

Next to Iguanodon, from Europe, Camptosaurus is the prototypical ornithopod. This dinosaur has been saddled by nature with a squat torso, a short tail, and a small, repulsive-looking head perched on the end of a thick neck. The only thing it has going for it is its occasional bipedal posture, which allows it to run away from predators at a respectable speed of fifteen or twenty miles per hour. Its intriguing name, which translates as "flexible lizard," refers to the presumed suppleness of this dinosaur's backbone, a misunderstanding perpetrated by the American paleontologist Othniel C. Marsh. In fact, Camptosaurus may have been one of the least flexible dinosaurs of the Jurassic period!

Camptosaurus is the ideal starting dinosaur for unseasoned field watchers, the equivalent of a Shetland pony for kids who aren't ready to ride an actual horse. The worst thing that will happen, if you venture too close to a grazing

herd, is that they'll see you coming and run away as fast as they can. Actually, check that: The worst thing that can happen is that you'll startle the herd, they'll run away as fast as they can, and the noise will attract the attention of a hungry Allosaurus, which will give up the chase and eat you instead. OK, let's start again: Assuming there are no Allosaurus in the immediate vicinity, Camptosaurus is the ideal starting dinosaur for unseasoned field watchers. That's our story, and we're sticking with it.

Castoroides (Giant Beaver)

Meaning of name: Beaver-like
Size: 8 feet long and 200 pounds
When it lived: Pleistocene (1 million to 10,000 years ago)
Where it lived: Midwestern and southeastern US
What it ate: Plants
Best viewed at: Field Museum of Natural History (Chicago)

During the late Pleistocene epoch—from about a million years ago to the cusp of the modern era—practically every mammal on earth grew to grotesquely comical sizes. Exhibit A is Castoroides, aka the Giant Beaver, which measured eight feet from head to tail and weighed in the neighborhood of two hundred pounds (the largest modern beavers, by contrast, top out at fifty or sixty pounds, max).

Everything else about the Giant Beaver was proportionately scaled as well, including its front teeth (which were almost six inches long) and its broad, flat tail (which hasn't preserved well in the fossil record but certainly was broader and flatter than the tails of any modern beaver).

The first question everybody asks upon hearing about the Giant Beaver is: Did it build equally giant dams? Well, before hearing the answer, you need to forget all those cartoon beavers you've ever seen building gigantic, Grand Cooley–type dams in the space of thirty seconds.

The fact is that beaver dams are rough-edged, ramshackle affairs that take anywhere from weeks to years to build, and are constructed not only out of sticks but stones, mud, leaves, and pretty much anything these industrious rodents can set their incisors on. Some Ohio residents claim

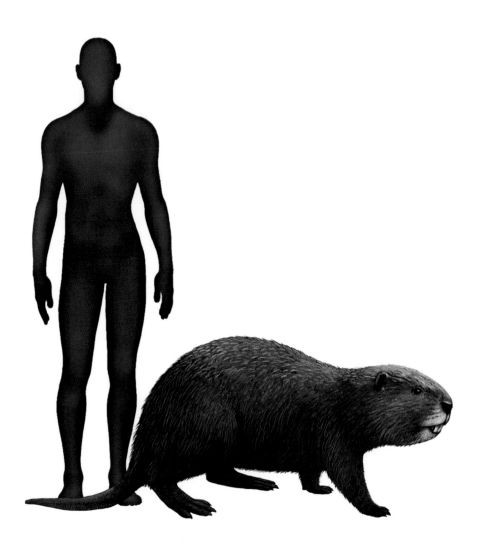

that an ancient, four-foot-high dam was erected by Giant Beavers, but since modern beavers have been known to build dams literally thousands of feet long and a dozen feet high, that hardly counts as conclusive evidence.

You can run into a Giant Beaver pretty much anywhere in the continental United States, but if you want to increase your odds, you're best off visiting the underside of the Great Lakes (Indiana and Ohio are the choice destinations of beaver cognoscenti) or the swamplands of Florida. You'll want to keep a respectful distance—after all, a full-grown Castoroides is about the size of a black bear—and whatever you do, don't pick up any stray sticks or lean against anything that looks even vaguely structural. There are few experiences in life more unpleasant than being wilded by a colony of angry, oversize beavers.

Centrosaurus

Meaning of name: Pointed lizard
Size: 20 feet long and 3 tons
When it lived: Late Cretaceous (75 million years ago)
Where it lived: Alberta Province, Canada
What it ate: Plants
Best viewed at: Dinosaur Provincial Park (Alberta, Canada)

Near the town of Hilda, in the southern part of Canada's Alberta province, is a sight that would make any dinosaur-lover's blood run cold. The Hilda Mega-Bonebeds, as they're called, contain the fragmented remains of nearly a thousand Centrosaurus individuals, which appear to have drowned while trying to cross a flooded river. (Whether this carnage happened all at once or during multiple crossings separated by years or even centuries remains unknown.) Since most ancient creatures are "diagnosed" on the basis

of one or two incomplete specimens, Centrosaurus may well be the best-attested dinosaur in the fossil record!

What do the Hilda Mega-Bonebeds tell us, apart from the fact that Centrosaurus wasn't a particularly accomplished swimmer?

Well, we can infer with virtual certainty that this ceratopsian (horned, frilled dinosaur) traversed the Canadian plains in vast herds consisting of hundreds of individuals. And the existence of these vast herds points to an evolutionary explanation for Centrosaurus's horns and frills: The horns were employed in intraspecies combat (that is, males with bigger horns had the opportunity to mate with more females) and the elaborate frills facilitated intra-herd recognition (allowing a baby Centrosaurus to quickly catch up with its mother).

And what was true for Centrosaurus was probably true for the dozens of other ceratopsian genera that roamed North America during the late Cretaceous period, including Triceratops (page 199), Pentaceratops (page 163), and Styracosaurus (page 196).

But let's not spend too much time mourning that unfortunate Centrosaurus herd. If you venture today into Alberta on a dinosaur-watching expedition, you're almost certain to spot a living, breathing Centrosaurus or two (or five, or a hundred), clustered peacefully around a watering hole or trudging north en masse in the course of their annual migration. Just be sure to remember that wherever there's a Canadian ceratopsian herd, a pack of hungry Albertosaurus (page 48) can't be far behind. You'll probably wind up being helicoptered out by the Canadian authorities, at your own expense, so be sure to carry your checkbook and a working cell phone.

Chasmosaurus

Meaning of name: Cleft lizard
Size: 15 feet long and 2 tons
When it lived: Late Cretaceous (75 million to 70 million years ago)
Where it lived: Alberta, Canada
What it ate: Plants
Best viewed at: Royal Tyrrell Museum (Drumheller, Canada), Canadian Museum of Nature (Ottawa, Canada)

It can get tedious out in the field tracking dinosaurs—which is why so many beginners insist on taking along their iPads, iPhones, portable DVD players, or whatever else they can think of to forget about the giant fireflies for two minutes and relax with an Adam Sandler movie. This is a bad idea, for two reasons: First, the glow of LCD screens has been known to attract hungry theropods, ranging from small, pesky dino-birds like Chirostenotes (page 90) to big, ravenous tyrannosaurs like Albertosaurus (page 48). And second, indulging in your portable electronics will cause you to completely neglect nature's version of the big screen, the giant display of Chasmosaurus.

A close relative of Centrosaurus (page 84), and similarly restricted to the vast flatlands of Alberta, Canada, Chasmosaurus is recognizable by its trio of not-very-impressive horns set under a huge, heart-shaped frill.

The horns were too short to have evolved for much more than sexual differentiation (perhaps Chasmosaurus males with sharper, more symmetrical horns had the opportunity to mate with more females), while the frill was too prominent (and too visible from literally miles away) not to have served some essential function. In fact, if a Chasmosaurus alpha spots you on a nearby mesa,

his frill will turn bright pink as its mesh of blood vessels engorges under the thin awning of skin, and the herd will trot away at triple speed (or perhaps even stampede in your direction, in which case you'd better get out of the way quick).

However, the frill of Chasmosaurus didn't evolve solely for signaling purposes. Paleontologists speculate that it served two other functions: to make this ceratopsian (horned, frilled dinosaur) look bigger from a distance, so a pack of Albertosaurus might think twice before barreling in for the kill, and (possibly) to help it gather in sunlight during the day and dissipate waste heat at night. (Like most ornithischian dinosaurs, Chasmosaurus was almost certainly cold-blooded and needed a reliable means to regulate its internal body temperature.) But all this is

mere biology. On your next dinosaur-watching expedition, leave your Samsung Galaxy at home and enjoy Chasmosaurus's gently psychedelic slide show instead.

Chirostenotes

Meaning of name: Narrow hands
Size: 7 feet long and 75 pounds
When it lived: Late Cretaceous (80 million to 75 million years ago)
Where it lived: Alberta, Canada
What it ate: Plants and bugs
Best viewed at: Royal Tyrrell Museum (Drumheller, Canada)

Chirostenotes is the Frankenstein monster of the dinosaur family, assembled, reassembled, and given new life by successive generations of paleontologists. This feathered dinosaur was "diagnosed" on the basis of a pair of fossilized hands discovered in 1914 in Alberta, Canada, but didn't receive the name Chirostenotes ("narrow hands") for another decade.

Shortly after that, a pair of feet was discovered in the same location, and then a partial jaw—the resulting dinosaurs being named Macrophalangia ("big toes") and Caenagnathus ("recent jaw"). It took until 1981 for experts to finally cobble these parts together, with the result that Chirostenotes, Macrophalangia, and Caenagnathus are now all considered to be the same dinosaur.

And what a strange dinosaur it is! Chirostenotes is a relative of Oviraptor, the notorious "egg thief" from central Asia who has gotten a bad rap (it turns out that the eggs it "stole" actually belonged to a brooding female). Feathered dinosaurs like Oviraptor were technically theropods—meaning they were close kin to meat-eaters like T. Rex (page 205) and Utahraptor (page 209)—but the family of oviraptors to which Chirostenotes belongs was probably omnivorous, or even exclusively herbivorous, and supplemented its diet with small insects and crustaceans. It's a bit

as if naturalists discovered a new breed of Brazilian jungle cat that subsisted on fruits and nuts rather than freshly killed rodents.

One good thing about Chirostenotes's all-purpose diet and relatively small size (only about seven feet long and seventy-five pounds) is that this dinosaur is easily approached in the wild, provided you hold out a big bowl of trail mix and don't mind returning to camp minus one or two fingers. If you and your party happen to be stranded and starving in the Canadian wilds, you may even be tempted to slaughter, pluck, and roast a trusting juvenile, with the proviso that you'll be taken into custody shortly afterward by wildlife protection authorities.

Coahuilaceratops

Meaning of name: Coahuila horned face
Size: 22 feet long and 4–5 tons
When it lived: Late Cretaceous (72 million years ago)
Where it lived: Northern Mexico/southern US
What it ate: Plants
Best viewed at: Museum of the Desert (Saltillo, Mexico), Utah Museum of Natural History (Salt Lake City)

Mexico isn't exactly well known for its dinosaurs: This country received the short end of the Cretaceous stick during the later Mesozoic era, when the huge island continent of Laramidia stretched all the way from Alberta, Canada, to New Mexico, with only its southernmost tip extending beyond the Mexican border. (Seventy-five million years ago, much of North America was covered by a shallow body of water known as the Western Interior Sea.)

And it's not as if the southernmost tip of Laramidia was a particularly hospitable environment to begin with. Paleontologists speculate that it was buffeted by violent storms and floods, making it a particularly difficult place for dinosaurs to secure a firm toehold.

That's where Coahuilaceratops comes into the picture. This is only the fourth dinosaur ever to be discovered in Mexico, and the very first

ceratopsian (the horned, frilled family of plant-eaters best characterized by Triceratops, page 199). The most distinctive feature of Coahuilaceratops is the four-foot-long brow horns sported by the males, which look like they're meant to deter predators but actually evolved for intraspecies combat (the same way bighorn rams head-butt each other for the right to mate with females).

Dinosaur-watchers agree that there are few sights more impressive than a pair of Coahuilaceratops alphas battling

into the sunset, their giant horns clacking and clattering in the desert air like oversize castanets.

You might imagine that Coahuilaceratops was the apex dinosaur of its ecosystem—this twenty-two-foot-long, five-ton ceratopsian was virtually immune to predation, since not even a natural enemy like Bistahieversor (page 69) would be foolish enough to take on a full-grown adult. That's not how nature works, though: While modern cheetahs wouldn't dare to tackle a three-ton elephant (even when hunting in packs), they have no compunction about picking off babies, juveniles, and sick, injured, or elderly adults. That, combined with the storms and floods mentioned above, helped keep the Coahuilaceratops population from growing too quickly and denuding southern Laramidia of its tasty vegetation.

Coelophysis

Meaning of name: Hollow form
Size: 7–9 feet long and 30–40 pounds
When it lived: Late Triassic/early Jurassic (200 million years ago)
Where it lived: Southwestern US
What it ate: Small animals
Best viewed at: New Mexico Museum of Natural History and Science (Albuquerque)

About sixty-five miles northwest of Santa Fe, nestled amidst rugged canyons and plateaus, lies a destination that's near and dear to the hearts of dinosaur lovers: Ghost Ranch, New Mexico. It was here, in 1947, that researchers stumbled upon the tangled remains of thousands of Coelophysis individuals.

While they were undoubtedly smarter than many of the other species in this book, these doomed meat-eaters didn't inhabit the Lost City of Dinosaurs, complete with paved streets, indoor plumbing, and Wi-Fi. Rather, it seems they were all caught in a flash flood some two hundred million years ago and their intertwined carcasses washed up in the same location.

Coelophysis is one of the few dinosaurs for which we have evidence of "robust" and "gracile" forms, one sex being about two feet longer and ten pounds heavier than the other. (One shouldn't conclude that the bigger individuals were necessarily male. After all, birds are descended from dinosaurs, and in many species the females are the showier gender!) Even more remarkably, from a taxonomic standpoint, Coelophysis wasn't all that far removed from the very first dinosaurs, which evolved in South America some fifteen million or twenty million years before—and which

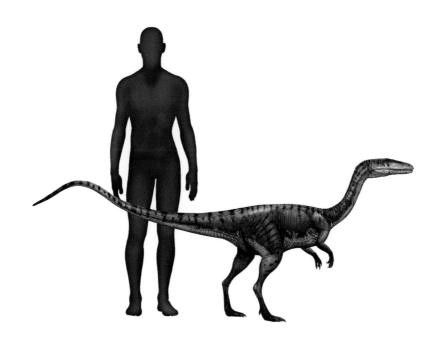

had spread not only to North America but to Africa and Eurasia by the start of the Jurassic period.

There's still a lot we don't know about the behavior of early theropods like Coelophysis, which is why extreme caution is called for out in the field. It's true that one, or even three or four, Coelophysis adults are unlikely to inflict any serious damage, considering that the "robust" form of this dinosaur was barely bigger than your average third-grader—but if twenty or thirty of these tiny terrors decide to swarm your Humvee at the same time, you may be in for some severe lacerations. It took one hundred million years for tiny bug-eaters like Coelophysis to evolve into ten-ton terrors like T. Rex, but the basic attributes of the breed—curiosity, hunger, and a distinct lack of empathy—were ineradicably programmed back in the Triassic wilds.

Deinonychus

Meaning of name: Terrible claw
Size: 12 feet long and 150 pounds
When it lived: Middle Cretaceous (110 million to 100 million years ago)
Where it lived: Western US
What it ate: Other dinosaurs
Best viewed at: Field Museum of Natural History (Chicago)

"They show extreme intelligence, even problem-solving intelligence. Especially the big one. We bred eight originally, but when she came in she took over the pride and killed all but two of the others. That one . . . when she looks at you, you can see she's working things out." That's Robert Muldoon, the rugged ranger of *Jurassic Park*, describing a caged pack of Velociraptors.

We have only two quibbles: first, *Jurassic Park*'s "Velociraptors" were actually modeled after the much more robust Deinonychus (Velociraptor, native to central Asia, was only slightly bigger than a chicken). And second, Muldoon vastly oversells the intelligence of his favorite dinosaurs, to the extent that, even today, people take it for granted that Deinonychus knew how to turn doorknobs. (We won't even mention the fact that this movie's heavies are depicted with green, scaly skin, when they were almost certainly covered with feathers.)

One thing is beyond dispute, however: Deinonychus was one of the most dangerous dinosaurs of the middle Cretaceous period, one hundred million years ago. The remains of this raptor have been found in close proximity to those of Tenontosaurus, a twenty-foot-long, two-ton duck-billed dinosaur, an unmistakable sign that Deinonychus hunted in packs.

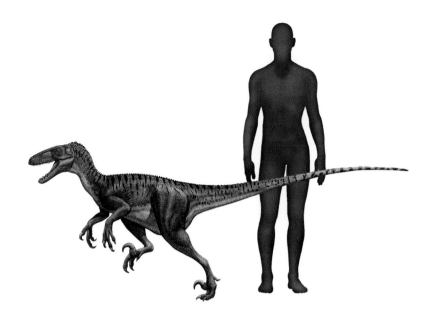

The chief weapon of this fearsome carnivore, besides its ornery disposition, was the single, oversize, curved claws on each of its hind feet, which it likely used to slash and disembowel its prey. To put it another way, if you're thinking about venturing out into the field and observing a pack of Deinonychus, don't, at least not without supplementing your life insurance first.

By the way, although it's not nearly as well known as Velociraptor (thanks again, *Jurassic Park*!), Deinonychus is the more important dinosaur from a scientific perspective. It was the discovery of various Deinonychus specimens in Montana during the 1960s that caused paleontologists to revise their perceptions of dinosaurs as huge, scaly, lumbering beasts. This was when the especially visionary scientist John Ostrom first mooted the idea that some dinosaurs might have been warm-blooded, and that birds might have descended from medium-size, feathered theropods like the "terrible claw."

Dilophosaurus

Meaning of name: Two-crested lizard
Size: 20 feet long and 1,000 pounds
When it lived: Early Jurassic (200 million to 190 million years ago)
Where it lived: Southwestern US
What it ate: Small animals
Best viewed at: Royal Tyrrell Museum (Drumheller, Canada), American Museum of Natural History (New York)

You thought *Jurassic Park* executed a hatchet job on Deinonychus (page 97)? That's nothing compared to the damage this movie wrought on Dilophosaurus, which has forever poisoned the public perception of this relatively innocuous theropod. The facts, in no particular order:

- In *Jurassic Park*, Dilophosaurus is depicted as being roughly the size of a golden retriever. In real life this dinosaur measured about twenty feet from head to tail and weighed in the vicinity of one thousand pounds. Not the kind of pooch you'd want to take to the dog park.

- In the movie, Dilophosaurus has a prominent neck frill, which (as Wayne Knight discovers to his displeasure) expands and flutters when it's about to attack. There is absolutely no evidence that Dilophosaurus (or any dinosaur, for that matter) had this kind of frill.

- Finally, and most egregiously, Dilophosaurus spits a wad of poison into Wayne Knight's eyes, temporarily blinding him. Not even close, and as made-up out of whole Jurassic cloth as anything in Steven Spielberg's blockbuster. Dinosaurs just didn't do this kind of thing.

So what's the big deal? Well, to this day nine out of ten people will tell you that Dilophosaurus was a garishly frilled, Labrador-size, poison-spitting menace. In fact, this dinosaur was something equally as interesting, if not quite as visually striking: a half-ton predator of early Jurassic Arizona, at a time when meat-eaters as a whole had yet to evolve to the striking proportions of the much later T. Rex (page 205). The only detail *Jurassic Park* got right was the paired crests atop this dinosaur's head, which may have been more prominent on males than on females (or vice-versa) and likely arose via sexual selection (that is, males

with bigger, more colorful crests had the opportunity to mate with more females).

So here's the bottom line: If you're headed out to the Sonoran desert to see a pack of Dilophosaurus, you can leave your protective rain gear and supply of antivenom behind. Just be sure to approach this dinosaur with the respect due to its half-ton bulk and perpetually wounded ego (how would you like to be described as a "little person" when you're actually six feet tall?), and you'll make it back to New Jersey with all your limbs intact.

Dimetrodon

Meaning of name: Two measures of teeth
Size: 11 feet long and 500 pounds
When it lived: Early Permian (280 million years ago)
Where it lived: South-central US
What it ate: Small animals
Best viewed at: Field Museum of Natural History (Chicago), American Museum of Natural History (New York)

"One of these things is not like the others. . . ." There's no prehistoric animal this *Sesame Street* tune applies to more aptly than Dimetrodon. Usually mistaken for a dinosaur, Dimetrodon actually dates to early Permian Texas and Oklahoma, at least forty million years before the first dinosaurs had even evolved (in South America).

If you must know, this sailed meat-eater was technically a pelycosaur, or "bowl lizard," an obscure family of reptiles that went on to spawn the therapsids, which themselves proceeded to evolve into the very first mammals of the early Triassic period. (Dinosaurs, by contrast, evolved from a different branch of reptiles, the archosaurs, or "ruling lizards," which also lay at the root of the pterosaur and crocodile family trees.)

Not only wasn't Dimetrodon really a dinosaur, but it was an order of magnitude smaller than famous dinosaurs like Triceratops (page 199) and Stegosaurus (page 193)—only about ten or eleven feet from head to tail and five hundred pounds. The feature that fools most people, in this regard, is Dimetrodon's prominent sail, which looks like it should be comparable in size to that of a full-grown Spinosaurus but really only boasts the surface area of a large umbrella. (Paleontologists aren't quite sure about

the function of this sail. Since Dimetrodon was undoubtedly cold-blooded, the most likely explanation is that it absorbed sunlight during the day and helped dissipate excess heat at night.)

Inexperienced dinosaur-watchers often mistake Dimetrodon for the closely related pelycosaur Edaphosaurus, which is about the same size and also sports a sail. The difference is that Dimetrodon is a carnivore, while Edaphosaurus is a confirmed plant-eater. If you're out on the Oklahoma plains and you see a squat, determined, sail-backed reptile slowly pursuing its equally squat, equally determined, and comparably sail-backed doppelganger, that's probably a Dimetrodon trying to brunch on its less-well-known cousin. Don't try to intervene (a hungry Dimetrodon, though fairly pokey, can be pretty mean) but marvel at nature's providence in providing even the slowest and clumsiest of its creations with the opportunity to land a square meal.

Diplodocus

Meaning of name: Double beam
Size: 100 feet long and 25 tons
When it lived: Late Jurassic (150 million years ago)
Where it lived: Western US
What it ate: Trees
Best viewed at: Carnegie Museum of Natural History (Pittsburgh, PA)

Diplodocus may be the most quintessentially American of all dinosaurs. Certainly, during the Mesozoic era, the United States teemed with all sorts of sauropods, theropods, ceratopsians, and raptors, but only Diplodocus was sponsored by a true plutocrat: the Pittsburgh industrialist Andrew Carnegie.

In the early twentieth century, Carnegie took it upon himself to commission a dozen plaster casts of this dinosaur's enormous skeleton, which he then donated to museums around the world (the original resides, naturally, in Pittsburgh's Carnegie Museum of Natural History).

Thanks to this benign act of cultural imperialism, Diplodocus is more closely identified with the United States than even T. Rex, even if most people still don't know how to pronounce its name (it's dip-LOW-doe-kuss, not dip-low-DOE-kuss).

Although it's essentially the same type of dinosaur as Brachiosaurus (page 72), Diplodocus differs in some important respects, which make all the difference when you're out observing in the field from three miles away. Diplodocus is slightly longer than Brachiosaurus (about one hundred feet from head to tail for an average specimen, with much of that taken up by its extra-long neck

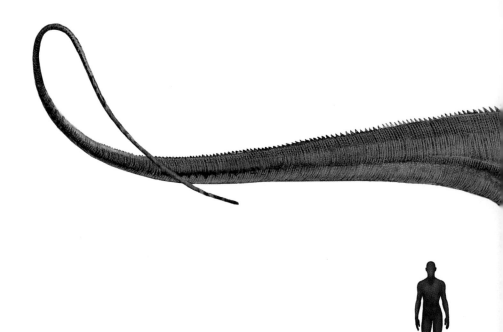

and tail), and, surprisingly, somewhat lighter, "only" about twenty-five tons.

More tellingly, the hind legs of Diplodocus are slightly longer than its front legs, giving it a parallel-to-the-ground posture markedly unlike that of Brachiosaurus (whose front legs are significantly longer than its hind legs). And like its close cousin Apatosaurus (page 60), Diplodocus has been known to whip its tail at supersonic speeds, which will produce quite the lethal gash in your Calvin Klein outerwear.

One of the issues that unceasingly baffles novice—and even experienced—dinosaur-watchers is the difference between Diplodocus, Supersaurus, and Seismosaurus. The impressively named Seismosaurus ("earthquake lizard") is 20 to 30 percent longer and heavier than Diplodocus, but

the weight of opinion today is that it's actually a superannuated Diplodocus individual (sauropods kept growing
for the entirety of their hundred-year life spans). Supersaurus, which sounds like it belongs in a comic book, was
about the same size as Seismosaurus and may also wind up
being lumped in with Diplodocus. (We won't even mention
Ultrasauros, formerly Ultrasaurus, which has since been
assigned to Supersaurus, which has since been assigned to
. . . well, you understand why paleontology can be such a
challenging profession.)

Dire Wolf

Size: 5 feet long and 150–200 pounds
When it lived: Pleistocene–Modern (one million to 10,000 years ago)
Where it lived: Canada, US, and Mexico
What it ate: Megafauna mammals
Best viewed at: George C. Page Museum (Los Angeles)

If you want to combine your mania for prehistoric animals with your unrequited love for Shia LeBeouf, Channing Tatum, and Scarlett Johansson, the Dire Wolf is the megafauna mammal for you.

The remains of *Canis dirus* have been dredged up by the thousands from the La Brea Tar Pits in Los Angeles, only a stone's throw from Hollywood, making it by far the best-represented mammal in the fossil record (even including another La Brea luminary, the Saber-Tooth Tiger, profiled on page 187). In a pop-culture crossover worthy of a studio PR wunderkind, Dire Wolves have even been featured on the HBO series *Game of Thrones*, though they're no match for Daenerys Targaryen's mythical dragons.

Unlike some other mega-beasts of the Pleistocene epoch—like the two-ton Australian wombat Diprotodon or our very own two-hundred-pound Giant Beaver (page 81)—the Dire Wolf wasn't significantly larger than modern wolves, and only about 25 percent bigger than huge domesticated canines like the American mastiff. However, *Canis dirus* was endowed with a more compact, muscular build, as well as a set of jaws and teeth that could easily crush the bones of a Woolly Mammoth (not that a pack of Dire Wolves was likely to take on a full-grown mammoth; this canine supplemented active hunting with opportunistic scavenging of already-dead creatures).

Technically, you may be impressed to learn that *Canis dirus* is classified as a "hypercarnivore," meaning it derived at least three-quarters of its nutritional requirements from bloody (and sometimes still-quivering) meat.

If you created a Venn diagram of "dog lovers" and "Dire Wolf–watchers," the intersection of these two sets might be labeled "mangled corpses awaiting dental identification by the LAPD." While Dire Wolves are technically canines, they're completely undomesticated and most likely completely undomesticatable—in fact, modern dogs descend from the late Pleistocene gray wolf, and if it had been remotely possible to tame a Dire Wolf, at least some tribe of early humans would have given it a shot. So no petting, no bone throwing, and no attempting to teach *Canis dirus* tricks—and whatever you do, don't get it in your mind to breed it with your Labradoodle to make a killing on the dog-breeding circuit.

Edmontosaurus

Meaning of name: Edmonton lizard
Size: 30 to 40 feet long and 3–4 tons
When it lived: Late Cretaceous (70 million to 65 million years ago)
Where it lived: Western US and Canada
What it ate: Plants
Best viewed at: Houston Museum of Natural Science (Houston), American Museum of Natural History (New York)

Edmontosaurus did not have an easy life. This gentle herbivore was preyed on by T. Rex (page 205) and Albertosaurus (page 48)—fossil specimens have been identified bearing the tooth marks of these ravenous predators—and it suffered from various types of cancer, as well as a painful condition called osteochondrosis, which interrupts the flow of blood through bone marrow.

However, before you envision a pathetic herd of bleeding, limping, mortally ill Edmontosaurus, bear in mind that this dinosaur's travails can be attributed entirely to the vagaries of the fossil record. There's no reason to believe that Edmontosaurus was more prone to illness than other dinosaurs. We just happen to have unearthed an unusual number of specimens bearing evidence of disease and disfigurement.

Classification-wise, Edmontosaurus was a classic hadrosaur, or duck-billed dinosaur, sporting a broad, flat, two-foot-long bill that wouldn't have looked out of place in an episode of *The Flintstones*. (A closely related genus, the even bigger Anatotitan, translates from the Greek as "giant duck.") Like other hadrosaurs, this dinosaur probably spent most of its day on all fours, browsing low vegetation, but was capable of running away on its hind legs

when threatened by the likes of T. Rex. Or rather, the full-grown, four-ton adults managed to run away, while smaller, shorter-legged hatchlings and juveniles, as well as the injured and diseased individuals described above, would have been unmercifully culled from the herd.

There's a special class of dinosaur-watchers specializing in Edmontosaurus, who are best compared to long-ago devotees of Phish and the Grateful Dead. Because Edmontosaurus is a migratory dinosaur—shuffling its way south at the end of summer to avoid the brutally cold temperatures and short days of the Arctic winter—you can gas up your RV, pack a month's supply of granola, and accompany the herd from a safe distance as it ambles from the northern reaches of Edmonton province to the balmier outskirts of Seattle.

Euoplocephalus

Meaning of name: Well-armored head
Size: 20 feet long and 2 tons
When it lived: Late Cretaceous (75 million years ago)
Where it lived: Western Canada and US
What it ate: Plants
Best viewed at: Royal Tyrrell Museum (Drumheller, Canada)

Imagine feeding an Ankylosaurus (page 57) a steady diet of steroids over the course of several years, and you might wind up with something like Euoplocephalus. Although Ankylosaurus outweighed its lesser-known cousin by almost a ton, Euoplocephalus was armored to an almost absurd degree; even its eyelids were covered by bony plates. And the tough dermal growths lining its head, back, and neck were pretty much impenetrable to bites from T. Rex and Albertosaurus (we won't even mention the heavy, blunt, hatchet-shaped club on the end of its swinging tail).

Long story short: While you and yours may be content riding around on an Ankylosaurus, you won't trust your kids' safety to anything less than a full-grown Euoplocephalus.

In fact, if life were fair, Euoplocephalus would be a far more popular dinosaur than Ankylosaurus. It's only a quirk of paleontology that Ankylosaurus was discovered and named first, on the basis of fairly limited fossil remains.

Euoplocephalus, by contrast, is represented by over forty nearly intact skeletons, a whopping fifteen of which still have their skulls (dinosaur heads, as a rule, don't tend to preserve well in the fossil record). All of these fossils were unearthed separately—not in a huge, tangled heap,

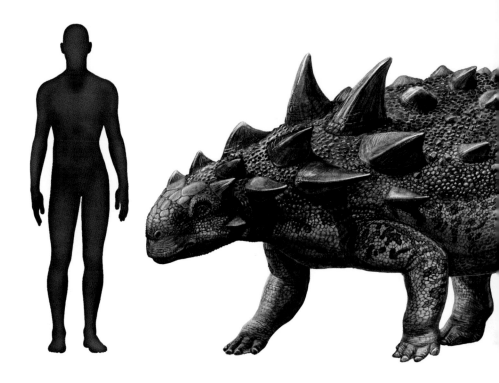

as is often the case with other plant-eating dinosaurs—a clue that Euoplocephalus was sufficiently well armored not to require the protection of a herd. In fact, an adult Euoplocephalus would have been virtually immune to predation; hatchlings and juveniles, by contrast, were less well-armored (since they needed room to grow) and had a much higher mortality rate.

As fascinating as any North American dinosaur of the late Cretaceous period, Euoplocephalus, sadly, can be a bit of a letdown out in the field—it's like watching a low-on-fuel Humvee crawling through your grandma's cabbage patch at three miles an hour. The exception is if you happen to catch this armored dinosaur in the act of mating, a spectacle that, to date, has evaded legions of devoted (and

prurient) dinosaur-watchers. Does the male Euoplocephalus actually climb onto the female's back? If so, how long does it take him to recover from his wounds? It's all a bit mysterious.

Hadrosaurus

Meaning of name: Sturdy lizard
Size: 30 feet long and 3–4 tons
When it lived: Late Cretaceous (80 million years ago)
Where it lived: Eastern US
What it ate: Plants
Best viewed at: Philadelphia Academy of Natural Sciences (Philadelphia)

The state of New Jersey isn't normally associated with dinosaurs, but back in its day, Hadrosaurus was as famous as any of the cast members of *Jersey Shore*. The scattered bones of this duckbill were discovered in 1838 by a New Jersey property owner, John Hopkins, who put them on informal display on the walls of his Haddonfield home. It

was only in 1858 that they were properly diagnosed and named by the eminent paleontologist Joseph Leidy.

In 1866 a second dinosaur, the tyrannosaur Dryptosaurus, was discovered in the Garden State by the equally eminent paleontologist Edward Drinker Cope. Since then, sadly, New Jersey's Mesozoic-era pickings have been practically nonexistent.

In 1868, after the dust kicked up by the Civil War had finally settled, Hadrosaurus became the first dinosaur ever to have its reconstructed bones exhibited to the American public, at the Philadelphia Academy of Natural Sciences. (Various dinosaur models were displayed at England's famous Crystal Palace Exhibition in 1854, including Iguanodon and Megalosaurus, but these fanciful reconstructions

weren't built around actual fossil casts.) That, unfortunately, represents the peak of Hadrosaurus's popularity. As more and more duck-billed dinosaurs were discovered in the American West, including the more striking Lambeosaurus (page 125) and Parasaurolophus (page 160), people forgot all about the Sturdy Lizard, even if it did lend its name to an entire family of plant-eating dinosaurs: the hadrosaurs.

Since Hadrosaurus is known from only a single, incomplete skeleton, there's a lot about this dinosaur that's left to the imagination. We can only guess, for example, whether Hadrosaurus traversed the eastern plains in massive herds or was more of a solitary vegetarian—or, for that matter, whether it possessed a prominent head crest (kind of the equivalent of the mullets sported by certain Jersey males) or had a more unprepossessing pate.

This is where amateur dinosaur-watchers can make a major contribution: If you're headed down to the Jersey Shore, and you see an unidentified dinosaur in the distance munching on a tasty conifer, take out your tablet and jot down every detail, no matter how seemingly insignificant. You might just land your own reality show on MTV!

Hyracotherium

Meaning of name: Hyrax-like beast
Size: 2 feet high and 50 pounds
When it lived: Early–middle Eocene (55 million to 45 million years ago)
Where it lived: Western US
What it ate: Plants
Best viewed at: National Museum of Natural History (Washington, DC)

Does the name Hyracotherium sound unfamiliar? Well, if you're of a certain age, you'll probably recognize this Eocene mammal as Eohippus, the "dawn horse," the distant, pint-size ancestor of Secretariat, Trigger, and the Budweiser Clydesdales.

There's a (not very interesting) story behind the change. A full forty years before Othniel C. Marsh erected the genus Eohippus, based on a fully articulated skeleton discovered on one of his western digs, the name Hyracotherium had been assigned to a fossil horse discovered in England. It turns out that Eohippus was probably the same animal as Hyracotherium, hence the reversion to the earlier name under the inflexible rules of paleontology.

We say "probably," because nothing in fossil hunting is written in stone (if you'll excuse the pun). Since horses indisputably evolved in North America and not Europe, it may yet turn out that the English species of Hyracotherium was a plain-vanilla "perissodactyl" (odd-toed ungulate) only distantly related to modern horses, while the American species (the former Eohippus) was the true progenitor, and thus deserving of restoration to genus status. In which case, forget everything you read in the paragraph above (we recommend the mind-wipe device from *Men in Black*)

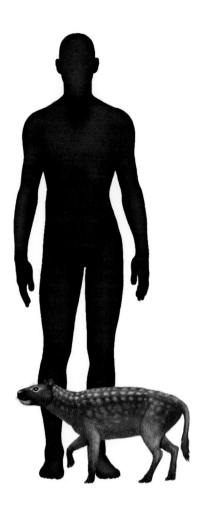

and be thankful we aren't discussing the Apatosaurus/
Brontosaurus brouhaha (page 60).

As important as it is in terms of equine evolution, Hyra-
cotherium/Eohippus can be a bit disappointing out in the
field. This ancestral horse is tiny (only about a foot and a
half high at the shoulder and fifty pounds soaking wet),
skittish, and easily mistaken for a deer. Its most notable feature—which you may just be able to make out with a pair
of binoculars—are its four-toed front feet and three-toed
back feet. In lieu of describing all the intermediate genera

between the erstwhile Eohippus and modern horses—Mesohippus, Parahippus, Epihippus, etc.—the story boils down to this: The descendants of Hyracotherium gradually lost their extra toes, increased in size, learned to digest grass, and spread across the western plains like wildfire. At that point horses vanished from North America entirely and had to be re-imported from Europe, but that's a subject for another book.

Kronosaurus

Meaning of name: Kronos lizard
Size: 30 feet long and 7 tons
When it lived: Middle Cretaceous (110 million years ago)
Where it lived: Oceans worldwide
What it ate: Fish, squids, and marine reptiles
Best viewed at: Harvard Museum of Natural History (Cambridge, MA)

Kronosaurus isn't a dinosaur. Rather, it's a type of marine reptile known as a pliosaur, and we have no direct evidence that it lived in North America.

So what, pray tell, is it doing in a book called *A Field Guide to the Dinosaurs of North America*? Well, for one thing, specimens of Kronosaurus have been discovered as far

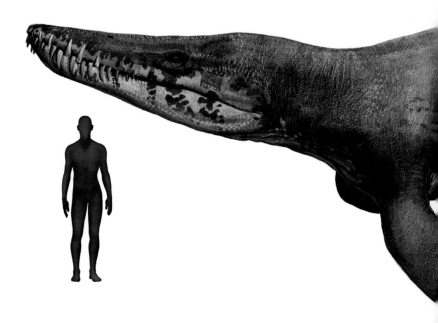

afield as Australia and South America, meaning this marine reptile probably had a worldwide distribution. For another thing, absence of evidence is not evidence of absence: For all we know, Kronosaurus plied the Western Interior Sea during the early Cretaceous period but didn't happen to leave any extant fossils. Third, and most important, the Kronosaurus on display at the Harvard Museum of Natural History is one of the seven wonders of the world, even if it's been inappropriately padded out with a couple of extra vertebrae.

Kronosaurus lived at a time when the world's oceans were dominated not by sharks (which did exist one hundred million years ago, albeit in relatively puny and insignificant forms) but by giant marine reptiles, which evolved

from terrestrial ancestors a few tens of millions of years before. Two related branches were the plesiosaurs and pliosaurs: The former possessed long necks, long flippers, and relatively streamlined bodies, while the latter (typified by Kronosaurus) were more compactly built, with huge teeth and jaws that wouldn't have looked out of place on a land-bound T. Rex. As fearsome as they were, though, pliosaurs were no match for the mosasaurs that evolved during the late Cretaceous period, streamlined killers like Plotosaurus (page 168) being the prime culprits in their eventual demise.

What should you do if you happen to be snorkeling in the Gulf of Mexico and you cross the wake of a full-grown Kronosaurus? Well, if the water is clear, the good news is that you'll be able to see this reptile approaching from a long way away. At thirty feet long and seven tons, it's kind of like being snuck up on by a small submarine. The not-so-good news is that Kronosaurus is about ten times bigger than the biggest great white sharks alive today, and twice the size of that fictional man-eater in *Jaws*—so if you're close enough to see it, you're close enough to be eaten by it.

Lambeosaurus

Meaning of name: Lambe's lizard
Size: 30 feet long and 4 tons
When it lived: Late Cretaceous (75 million to 70 million years ago)
Where it lived: Western US and Canada
What it ate: Plants
Best viewed at: Royal Ontario Museum (Toronto, Canada), American Museum of Natural History (New York)

It's impossible to discuss Lambeosaurus without giving a shout-out to the man after whom this dinosaur was named, Lawrence M. Lambe, one of the lesser-known figures in the history of paleontology. Working for the Geological Survey of Canada at the turn of the twentieth century, Lambe discovered, publicized, and mounted for exhibition many of the dinosaurs discovered in Alberta province and described in this book, and was responsible for naming Edmontosaurus (page 111), Euoplocephalus (page 113), Centrosaurus (page 84), and Chasmosaurus (page 87). Despite what many people think, Lambe didn't name Lambeosaurus after himself. That was an honor paid by another Canadian paleontologist, William Parks, in 1923.

As far as Lambeosaurus itself is concerned, this hadrosaur (duck-billed dinosaur) was distinguished by the oddly shaped crest on its head—which looked like an upside-down hatchet, was bigger in males than in females, and was probably used to funnel blasts of air for communication purposes.

There were lots of comparably sized hadrosaurs shuffling across the plains of western North America during the late Cretaceous period, so it only makes sense that they differentiated to help facilitate intra-herd recognition. (The

crest of Lambeosaurus changed in shape and size as this
dinosaur aged, which once prompted unwitting paleontologists to assign the juveniles to new genera. Some now-
discarded names for this hadrosaur include Trachodon,
Tetragonosaurus, and Procheneosaurus.)

The good thing about Lambeosaurus, as far as dinosaur-
watchers are concerned, is that this four-ton hadrosaur
will be way too busy shoveling leaves into its gaping maw

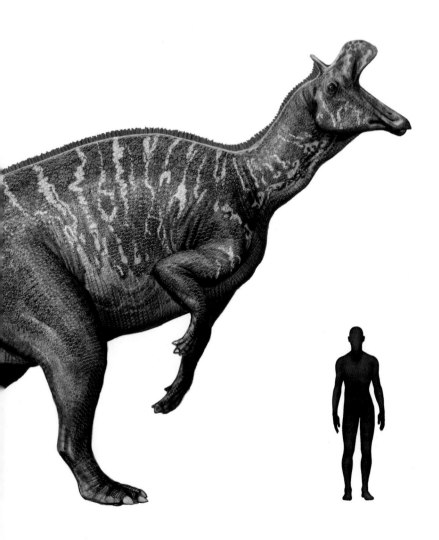

to notice you lurking in the distance with your binoculars. But if you do happen to startle a member of the herd, get ready for quite a sight and quite a sound. Like other duck-bills, Lambeosaurus was capable of running away on two legs, which must have looked like an oversize, buff Barney attempting to do the hundred-yard dash whilst shouting at the top of his big purple lungs.

Maiasaura

Meaning of name: Good mother lizard
Size: 30 feet long and 4 tons
When it lived: Late Cretaceous (80 million to 75 million years ago)
Where it lived: Western US
What it ate: Plants
Best viewed at: Royal Ontario Museum (Toronto, Canada)

If you look closely at its name, you'll notice that Maiasaura is the only dinosaur in this book to end with an "-a" rather than the usual "-us." You can thank two hundred years of paleontological sexism: The vast majority of dinosaurs, like Allosaurus (page 51) and Camptosaurus (page 78), are named after the male of the species, for the simple reason that most early fossil hunters were male. Maiasaura, the "good mother lizard," carries the feminine suffix because most of the identified specimens of this dinosaur, discovered in close proximity to their eggs, appear to have been female. (This imbalance is slowly being rectified. In the last few years, politically correct paleontologists have added

Bonitasaura, Gasparinisaura, and Leaellynasaura to the dinosaur bestiary.)

Not only is Maiasaura the first described "female" dinosaur but, in the late 1970s, the discovery of Montana's "Egg Mountain"—which has yielded the fossils of dozens of Maiasaurus adults, juveniles, and hatchlings—provided the first proof that some dinosaurs actually cared for their young after they hatched, rather than simply abandoning them to the cruelty of nature.

Maiasaura females tended to their young in circular clutches, containing about thirty to forty eggs apiece,

which were kept warm not by this dinosaur's body heat (no one wants to be sat on by a four-ton hadrosaur!) but by rotting vegetation. As the eggs hatched and the helpless baby dinosaurs slowly developed their land legs, hungry predators would be kept at bay by the protective instincts of two or three hundred agitated Maiasaura adults.

If you decide to visit the Two Medicine Formation in Montana, where Egg Mountain is located, use the same common sense you'd display if you came upon a mother grizzly bear and her newborn cubs. Strike your campsite a respectable distance from the nearest clutch and raise your binoculars slowly and unthreateningly, lest you trigger the alarm of an edgy female. And whatever you do, if an adorable baby Maiasaura somehow escapes the nest and waddles in your direction, don't attempt to pick it up, much less strap it into your kid's car seat and take it back to "civilization." Your liability policy won't cover a Maiasaura mom throwing herself on the roof of your SUV and flattening its occupants.

Medusaceratops

Meaning of name: Medusa horned face
Size: 20 feet long and 2 tons
When it lived: Late Cretaceous (78 million years ago)
Where it lived: Western US
What it ate: Plants
Best viewed at: Wyoming Dinosaur Center (Thermopolis)

You might think North America is best represented in the dinosaur record books by tyrannosaurs like T. Rex (page 205) or sauropods like Diplodocus (page 105), but pound for pound, the horned, frilled herbivores known as ceratopsians may have been the most common land animals of the late Cretaceous period.

A bewildering array of these dinosaurs has been discovered over the past few decades, differentiated by strange admixtures of overall size, territory, and the size, shape, and ornamentation of their horns and frills. Some ceratopsians—like Agujaceratops (page 45) and Coahuilaceratops (page 92)—roamed the American Southwest, while others, like Medusaceratops, inhabited the more familiar haunts of the western United States (in this case, the state of Montana).

As you might already have guessed, Medusaceratops was named after the Medusa, the monster of Greek myth with snakes for hair and a gaze that turned men to stone—not because this dinosaur was dangerous to look at, but because the curlicues sprouting from its massive frill looked uncannily like coiled snakes.

But wait, it gets better: The full name of this ceratopsian is *Medusaceratops lokii*, the species name honoring Loki, the Norse god of mischief. That's because, when the fossil of Medusaceratops was excavated from a bone bed abutting northern Montana's Milk River, researchers had no idea what kind of dinosaur they were dealing with. (The specifics of ceratopsian morphology can be a bit dry, but in layman's terms, Medusaceratops was an early "chasmosaurine" ceratopsian with some disturbingly "centrosaurine" characteristics.)

If you're planning a trip to Montana to see this exotic new dinosaur, keep in mind that Medusaceratops is a herd

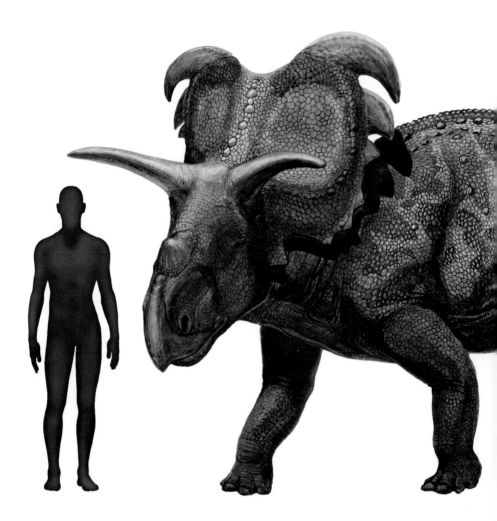

animal, meaning that if you venture too close (or otherwise betray your presence, say, by turning up the volume on your iPod), you may find yourself on the wrong end of a brainless stampede. Also, Medusaceratops hatchlings and juveniles tend to attract the attention of carnivorous dinosaurs, though exactly what kind remains a mystery (to date, we don't know of any associated tyrannosaurs that lived in this specific region of Montana seventy-eight million years ago). Keep your eyes peeled, your camera ready, and your SUV fueled, in case you live to tell the tale and want to sell your million-dollar snapshot to *Reckless Adventurer* magazine.

Megalonyx

Meaning of name: Giant claw
Size: 10 feet long and 1 ton
When it lived: Pleistocene–Modern (2 million to 10,000 years ago)
Where it lived: Woodlands of North America
What it ate: Plants
Best viewed at: Natural History Museum of Utah (Salt Lake City), American Museum of Natural History (New York)

Plenty of megafauna mammals lived in North America during the Pleistocene epoch, but only one of them has the honor of being named by Thomas Jefferson. In 1797, when he was serving as vice president of the American Philosophical Society, Jefferson came into possession of scattered bones that had been recovered from a cave in Virginia. Misinterpreting the specimen as an extant (but still undiscovered) species of lion, Jefferson named it Megalonyx ("giant claw") and even asked Lewis and Clark to keep their eyes peeled for this elusive beast during their famous westward journey.

A couple of years later, it was determined that the bones actually belonged to a giant sloth, and it took twenty years after that for Megalonyx to become an official part of the Pleistocene bestiary.

Although it ranged far and wide across North America—fossils have been discovered in Idaho, Nevada, Texas, and even Florida—Megalonyx originated in South America, which was cut off from the mainstream of evolution for much of the Cenozoic era. Even before the formation of the Isthmus of Panama—which connected North America and South America shortly before the start of the Pleistocene epoch—the ancestors of the Giant Ground Sloth

"island-hopped" their way to North America, a process that took hundreds of thousands, if not millions, of years. (What that means is that the sloths blundered their way atop a raft-size tangle of sticks, floated to a nearby island, and bred to their heart's content—and that their descendants repeated the process, island by island, over the course of generations.)

At ten feet long and one ton, Megalonyx was far from the biggest prehistoric sloth—that honor belongs to the two-ton Megatherium ("giant beast") of South America— but it was still much, much bigger than any sloth alive today.

By the start of the modern era, about ten thousand years ago, sloths had vanished from North America, but don't give up all hope for your Megalonyx-watching expedition. It's possible that a few poky individuals still persist in the Appalachian woodlands, too dumb to know they're supposed to be extinct, and too slow to have made it down to Cabo San Lucas even with a two-millennium head start. Just keep your distance, because these oversize sloths may have supplemented their vegetarian diets with occasional servings of fresh meat.

Megapnosaurus

Meaning of name: Big dead lizard
Size: 6 feet long and 75 pounds
When it lived: Early Jurassic (200 million to 180 million years ago)
Where it lived: Western US
What it ate: Small animals
Best viewed at: New Mexico Museum of Natural History and Science (Albuquerque)

More so than with any other dinosaur in this book, we feel firmly confident in saying that Megapnosaurus no longer exists. For decades, this slender meat-eater was known as Syntarsus, a name under which it appeared in countless kids' books of the 1960s and 1970s, until it was discovered that the name Syntarsus had already been assigned to an obscure genus of beetle.

In 2001 Syntarsus was renamed Megapnosaurus, or "big dead lizard," which was a bit of an in-joke among paleontologists—but the joke was on them, because most of their colleagues had already decided that Syntarsus, aka Megapnosaurus, was really a species of Coelophysis (page 95)!

Why go into so much detail about a dinosaur that so few people even recognize, much less agree about? Well, the fact is that this is far from an uncommon situation. Prehistoric animals are being reassessed all the time, and there have been countless instances in which a well-known dinosaur was "downgraded" to a species (or a specimen) of a preexisting genus. Other, more recent, examples include *Dracorex hogwartsia*, the widely touted "Harry Potter" dinosaur that may actually have been a juvenile Pachycephalosaurus (page 154), and Torosaurus, which was almost certainly a superannuated Triceratops (page 199).

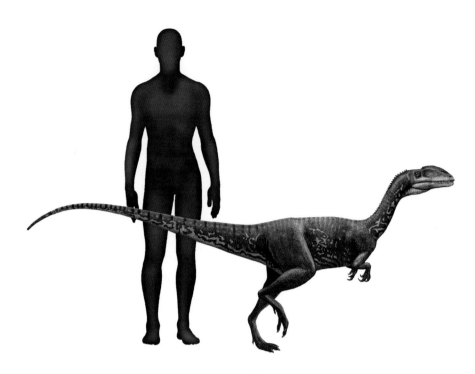

All that said, what should you expect if you encounter Megapnosaurus, aka Syntarsus, aka Coelophysis, out in the field? Unless you bring your night-vision goggles, you may be in for a disappointment: There's reason to believe this dinosaur is exclusively nocturnal, the giveaway being the "scleral rings" around its eyes similar to those of modern, night-hunting birds. You're also likely to encounter Megapnosaurus, et al, in fairly large packs—over two dozen individuals have been recovered from a quarry in Zimbabwe, Africa, where this dinosaur also lived—so it's not a good idea to stray too far from your SUV, or to call unnecessary attention to the fact that its trunk is loaded with hamburgers and chicken wings for that big post-expedition cookout.

Nanotyrannus

Meaning of name: Tiny tyrant
Size: 17 feet long and 1,000 pounds
When it lived: Late Cretaceous (70 million years ago)
Where it lived: Western US
What it ate: Other dinosaurs
Best viewed at: Burpee Museum of Natural History (Rockford, IL), Rocky Mountain Dinosaur Resource Center (Woodland Park, CO)

Sometimes, a name is just so perfect that it takes precedence over messy details like provenance and fossil evidence. Such is the case with Nanotyrannus, the "tiny tyrant," which was initially described as a juvenile specimen of Gorgosaurus when its skull was discovered in 1948. It was then elevated to genus status forty years later by, among other paleontologists, Robert T. Bakker (a technical adviser for *Jurassic Park*).

What prompted the reassessment was that the pieces of this tyrannosaur's skull appeared to be fused, a characteristic of adult, not juvenile, dinosaurs. Unfortunately, another examination ten years later showed that the skull wasn't fully fused after all and probably belonged to a subadult tyrannosaur.

In most cases that would be the end of the story: Nanotyrannus would be acknowledged as an honest mistake, and the type fossil would be reclassified as a Gorgosaurus juvenile. However, the "tiny tyrant" secured a hold on the public's imagination, with the result that Nanotyrannus has hovered on the fringes of paleontological respectability for the last three decades.

Today, most experts believe that Nanotyrannus was a juvenile, not of Gorgosaurus but of none other than

Tyrannosaurus Rex (page 205). The snag, however, is that its skull is packed with about a half-dozen extra teeth.

So, did T. Rex juveniles lose their teeth as they aged? It's not inconceivable, since the same has been known to happen with the closely related tyrannosaur Gorgosaurus. There's also a small pit in the back of Nanotyrannus's skull that hasn't been observed in other tyrannosaurs, which may be the only thing keeping it in the dinosaur record books!

But let's not quibble about whether Nanotyrannus deserves genus status or is actually a glorified T. Rex. The question is, if you see one stomping in the distance during your Utah motorcade, what should you do? At a mere seventeen feet long and one thousand pounds, Nanotyrannus is unlikely to build up a head of steam and tip over your

Trailblazer like its dad (or uncle) did in *Jurassic Park*. On the other hand, not even the biggest grizzly weighs half a ton, and you wouldn't get out of your car and hand-feed Yogi Bear.

Our advice: Lock your doors, clean your zoom lens, and snap as many pictures as you can before you attract the Nano's attention. With any luck, your photographic evidence will help scientists decide whether this controversial dinosaur actually exists.

Nothronychus

Meaning of name: Sloth claw
Size: 15 feet long and 1 ton
When it lived: Late Cretaceous (90 million years ago)
Where it lived: Southwestern US
What it ate: Plants, possibly some meat as well
Best viewed at: Natural History Museum of Utah (Salt Lake City)

During the Mesozoic era, pretty much every type of dinosaur that lived in Eurasia had its counterpart in North America—which makes sense, because these two continents were joined together in the giant landmass of Laurasia for more than one hundred million years.

The list includes tyrannosaurs (Alioramus in Asia vs. T. Rex in North America), raptors (Velociraptor and Deinonychus), and giant, plant-eating sauropods and ornithopods. One puzzling exception, until recently, was the breed of feathered dinosaurs known as therizinosaurs, after the most famous genus, Therizinosaurus. With their long feathers, bipedal postures, pot bellies, and cartoonishly long claws, therizinosaurs looked like the badly costumed villains from a long-forgotten episode of *Scooby Doo, Where Are You?*

For decades experts surmised that therizinosaurs were an evolutionary aberration confined to central Asia. At least that was what they surmised until 2001, when a team of researchers discovered the "type specimen" of Nothronychus in the Zuni Basin of New Mexico. Even still, there remained a lingering whiff of disbelief until Falcarius, a second genus of North American therizinosaur, was unearthed in Utah a few years later. (The fossil evidence adds up nicely: The thirteen-foot-long, five-hundred-pound

Falcarius preceded the fifteen-foot-long, one-ton Nothronychus by about forty million years.)

Even more tellingly, these North American therizino-
saurs inhabited the same stark, semiarid plains as their
Asian counterparts, which prowled the fringes of the Gobi
Desert.

One of the mysterious things about Nothronychus,
which will have a direct bearing on how you choose to
approach it in the wild, is its diet. Technically, Nothronychus

is a theropod, the widespread family of bipedal dinosaurs that includes tyrannosaurs, raptors, and feathered dino-birds. The vast majority of theropods are confirmed meat-eaters, while Nothronychus and its therizinosaur ilk, with their scythe-shaped claws, seem to be adapted to munching on vegetation—though it's not inconceivable that they enjoy chowing down on the occasional tasty carcass as well.

Ojoceratops

Meaning of name: Ojo horned face
Size: 20 feet long and 2–3 tons
When it lived: Late Cretaceous (70 million years ago)
Where it lived: Southwestern US
What it ate: Plants
Best viewed at: Nowhere yet

After Agujaceratops (page 45) and Coahuilaceratops (page 92), we've included Ojoceratops in this book as the third in our trio of southwestern ceratopsians, to drive home the point that watching dinosaurs is a lot like watching birds. (Ironically, birds evolved from saurischian dinosaurs like theropods and sauropods, rather than ornithischian dinosaurs like ceratopsians, but don't let that odd fact disconcert you overmuch.)

Just as you might struggle to distinguish a pine siskin from a common redpoll, so you may throw up your hands and claim that Ojoceratops looks "just like" Triceratops (page 199), even though paleontologists have determined (at least for now) that it merits its own genus.

It's true that Ojoceratops looks a lot like Triceratops, which is much better known to the general public and much easier to see in person (Ojoceratops has yet to crack the museum circuit). But the fact is that Ojoceratops lived a few million years before Triceratops and a few hundred miles away, in the southwestern (rather than classically western) United States.

Although its paired brow horns were similar to those of Triceratops, the frill of Ojoceratops was more modest and rounded. Ironically (again!) Ojoceratops was "diagnosed" from a set of fossil remains once assigned

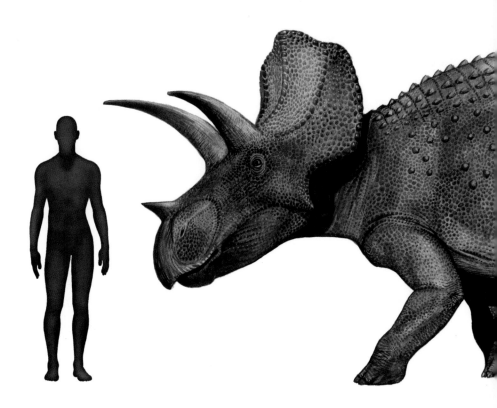

to Torosaurus, a genus that is now considered synony-
mous with Triceratops—and there's word afoot that the
"Ojo horned face" may have been the same dinosaur as
Eotriceratops, or the "dawn Triceratops," native to Alberta,
Canada.

OK, OK, you're right: Maybe dinosaur watching is much
more complicated than bird watching. Right now you're
probably thinking, "I don't care if Ojoceratops was really
a species of Triceratops, Eotriceratops or Torosaurus. I just
want to know what I should do if it pounds on the door of
my SUV!" Well, like any ceratopsian, Ojoceratops is unlikely
to give you any real trouble; this dinosaur just wants to be

left alone to feed to its heart's content, and a herd will only stampede if inadvertently threatened (so don't let your four-year-old play with your car horn while you and your spouse take a closer look).

Ophthalmosaurus

Meaning of name: Eye lizard
Size: 20 feet long and 2 tons
When it lived: Late Jurassic (165 million to 150 million years ago)
Where it lived: Shallow seas of North America
What it ate: Fish and marine reptiles
Best viewed at: American Museum of Natural History (New York)

You don't have to be an ophthalmologist to appreciate Ophthalmosaurus, the "eye lizard," though it would sure help you to pronounce its name. This ichthyosaur (a family of marine reptiles likely spawned by the same Triassic

archosaurs that gave rise to the dinosaurs) had a near-worldwide distribution during the late Jurassic period.

Ophthalmosaurs prowled the shores of the northern supercontinent Laurasia, which later broke apart into North America and Eurasia. Like other "fish lizards" of its day, this marine reptile looked uncannily like a modern dolphin or bluefin tuna, an example of the tendency of nature to evolve the same body plans in response to the same evolutionary constraints.

As you may already have guessed, the most distinctive feature of Ophthalmosaurus was its eyes—which were four inches in diameter and supported by bony structures

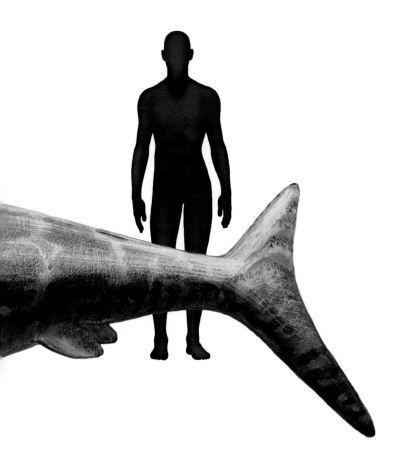

called "sclerotic rings." Clearly, as a deep-sea feeder, Ophthalmosaurus needed to gather in as much sunlight as possible and keep its oversize eyes from being mashed into jelly by the extreme water pressure.

Like all marine reptiles, Ophthalmosaurus breathed air, but it may have been capable of staying underwater for as long as twenty minutes at a stretch—and in case you still doubt this ichthyosaur's deep-sea-diving bona fides, some fossil specimens bear skeletal evidence of the bends, the only explanation being that these individuals were chased out of the deep by even bigger predators and had to ascend quickly in order to avoid getting eaten.

If you're not mentally prepared, encountering an Ophthalmosaurus on a snorkeling expedition can be an unnerving experience—imagine if that giant shark from *Jaws* had grapefruit-size peepers and an even nastier disposition. If you suspect you're venturing into ichthyosaur-infested waters, you'll need the protection of a sturdy cage, but whatever you do, don't take along your undersea flashlight. There's nothing that annoys an Ophthalmosaurus more than being suddenly blinded by a five-hundred-watt beam—in the course of thrashing around, it will demolish your cage, your harpoon gun, and your internal organs, not to mention every single hired hand aboard your chartered fishing boat.

Ornithomimus

Meaning of name: Bird mimic
Size: 11 feet long and 350–400 pounds
When it lived: Late Cretaceous (75 million to 65 million years ago)
Where it lived: American West
What it ate: Small animals and vegetation
Best viewed at: Royal Ontario Museum (Toronto, Canada)

Of all the prehistoric animals in this book, Ornithomimus may prove the most challenging to your top-of-the-line digital camera. This dinosaur has been known to run at a blazing forty or fifty miles per hour, not only for short stretches but for minutes at a time—which helps explain why it doesn't usually feature on the dinner menu of T. Rex (page 205) or Albertosaurus (page 48).

As it streaks, roadrunner-like, across your field of vision, you may notice how uncannily Ornithomimus resembles an ostrich, complete with long neck, long legs, small head, and prominent feathers. (And not only Ornithomimus— other "bird mimic" dinosaurs also sport this fashionable look, including Gallimimus, the chicken mimic; Pelecanimimus, the pelican mimic; and, of course, Struthiomimus, the ostrich mimic.)

One of the strangest things about Ornithomimus—and one of the most dangerous things, from the perspective of a novice dinosaur-watcher—is that it's technically a theropod (the line of meat-eating dinosaurs that includes Deinonychus and Allosaurus) but enjoys an omnivorous diet. In fact, like your average barnyard chicken, Ornithomimus will eat anything and everything it can fit into its small, toothless beak, including bugs, nuts, fruits, small birds and

lizards, and the fingers of people who unwisely approach it holding a tray of cocktail wieners.

It's not unknown for a particularly hungry Ornithomimus to strap on the afterburners and chase small, skittering animals into the underbrush—a good reason not to bring your shih tzu along on your trip.

One thing we don't yet know is whether Ornithomimus and pals not only look like big chickens but taste like big chickens as well. As you're no doubt aware, the rules

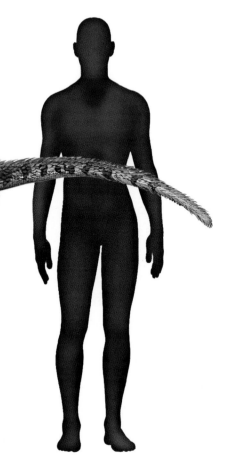

of the International Dinosaur Watchers Convention specifically prohibit killing and eating animals out in the field, and any recently deceased corpses you come across will long since have been hollowed out by opportunistic scavengers. Even if you did take it in mind to go all Food Network on an unwary Ornithomimus, it would zoom away like Usain Bolt on steroids as soon as it saw you approaching with that knife and fork. Our advice: Leave the chicken dinners to the folks at Perdue, and enjoy looking at, but don't try to touch or pluck, Ornithomimus and its fine feathered friends.

Pachycephalosaurus

Meaning of name: Thick-headed lizard
Size: 15 feet long and 1,000 pounds
When it lived: Late Cretaceous (65 million years ago)
Where it lived: Western US
What it ate: Plants
Best viewed at: Royal Ontario Museum (Toronto, Canada)

"The first rule of Fight Club is: You do not talk about Fight Club." To no dinosaur does this famous quote more aptly apply than Pachycephalosaurus, a big-domed plant eater that clearly engages in some kind of fighting behavior but has yet to be directly observed doing so.

The most notable feature of Pachycephalosaurus is the ten-inch-thick mound of bone on top of its skull, which clearly didn't evolve to protect this dinosaur's tiny brain (if that were the case, this feature would have evolved in numerous species), which suggests that it must serve some other purpose. Adding to the mystery, many fossilized Pachycephalosaurus skulls bear evidence of infections and lesions, so clearly this dinosaur wasn't using its plus-size dome to do math problems.

There are two competing theories. The first is that Pachycephalosaurus males wield their thick skulls the same way bullhorn sheep wield their knobby horns: to head-butt each other at high speed, the winner securing dominance in the herd and the right to mate with females. (Think of how college guys might behave in a bar on a Saturday night.)

The second camp says high-speed head-butting would be sheer suicide, and Pachycephalosaurus uses its noggin in more measured fashion, to butt the flanks of unruly herd

members and (just possibly) nosy predators like T. Rex. In any event, we do know that Pachycephalosaurus's skull got increasingly thick as this dinosaur aged, but that fact can be used to support either theory.

If only someone, anyone, could catch Pachycephalosaurus in the act of defending itself or asserting its dominance! Unfortunately, a whole subculture of thick-headed-dinosaur enthusiasts has been distracted by another enduring controversy, which is just how many of these strange plant-eaters there actually are prowling the American West.

In recent years two different dinosaurs, Stygimoloch and Dracorex, have been reinterpreted as juvenile growth stages of Pachycephalosaurus. The same fate may yet befall two other, smaller pachycephalosaurs from Asia, Goyocephale and Homalocephale. Anyway, if you do happen to catch a pair of Pachycephalosaurus males getting in each others' faces, try to capture as much video footage as you can—but don't let anyone in on the secret.

Pachyrhinosaurus

Meaning of name: Thick-nosed lizard
Size: 20 feet long and 2–3 tons
When it lived: Late Cretaceous (70 million years ago)
Where it lived: Western US
What it ate: Plants
Best viewed at: Perot Museum of Nature and Science (Dallas)

All sorts of unsavory stories are making the rounds about why Pachyrhinosaurus, rather than Triceratops, was cast as the star of the late, unlamented movie *Walking with Dinosaurs 3D.*

Was the BBC paid off by a natural history museum hoping to promote its collection of Pachyrhinosaurus specimens? Was there some kind of giant casting couch involved—a no-pay, no-play proposition by a sleazy producer? Whatever the case, Pachyrhinosaurus, and not its more famous rival, got star billing.

You have to admit, Pachyrhinosaurus is a pretty unprepossessing heartthrob. This ceratopsian (horned, frilled dinosaur) lacks any horns to speak of, with only a tiny pair jutting out from the top of its not-very-prominent frill, compared to the two robust, dangerous-looking weapons wielded by Triceratops. What Pachyrhinosaurus does have is a thick, ugly nose (more of a protuberance, really), which is sometimes employed in intraspecies combat but mainly serves to funnel loud blasts of sound, kind of like hearing Jimmy Durante sneeze from half a mile away. (If you're one of the three people who actually saw *Walking with Dinosaurs 3D* in theaters, you should know that female Pachyrhinosaurus juveniles weren't actually tinted pink, but you may have figured that out for yourself.)

Perhaps the most disappointing thing about Pachyrhinosaurus is that everything you could possibly know about it has already been covered by the other, more interesting ceratopsians in this book—not only Triceratops, but Chasmosaurus (page 87), Pentaceratops (page 163), even the relatively obscure Coahuilaceratops (page 92) and Ojoceratops (page 145).

Long story short: You're most likely to encounter Pachyrhinosaurus in herds, which was the most effective way

to keep large predators at bay during the late Cretaceous period. And at any given moment, it will likely be eating or dozing, to the exclusion of more interesting activities like fighting or running away from a hungry T. Rex.

Parasaurolophus

Meaning of name: Near-crested lizard
Size: 30 feet long and 3 tons
When it lived: Late Cretaceous (70 million years ago)
Where it lived: Western US and Canada
What it ate: Plants
Best viewed at: Royal Ontario Museum (Toronto, Canada)

So you're out in the middle of the South Dakota Badlands, craggy, treacherous plateaus as far as the eye can see and not another human being within fifty miles. Suddenly you hear what sounds like an enormous downtown Chicago traffic jam: honking, bellowing, the deep, skin-crawling rumble of three-ton semis.

Are you running low on food and water and experiencing hallucinations? Did you make a wrong turn at Albuquerque? No, you're simply about to encounter one of the wonders of nature: a panicked herd of Parasaurolophus being chased in your direction by a rampaging T. Rex. Nothing at all to worry about, right? Just go on doing whatever it was you were doing.

Probably the loudest dinosaur on the face of the earth—if you exclude its slightly bigger Asian cousin, Charonosaurus—Parasaurolophus can be recognized by the huge, narrow, backward-curving crest on the top of its head. Partly hollow on the inside, like a tenor saxophone or a didgeridoo, this crest funnels blasts of snorted air to produce some truly unnerving sounds—imagine Spinal Tap if their amplifiers really did go up to eleven.

Some scientists speculate that the crests of Parasaurolophus serve a dual purpose—perhaps they help to cool this dinosaur's massive head, or aid in intraspecies recognition, or even allow this hadrosaur to breathe underwater for short periods of time—but in the midst of all that incessant noise, these experts have had a hard time making themselves heard.

One of the curious (and confusing) things about Parasaurolophus is that it has been named with reference to other North American duck-billed dinosaurs to which it's only remotely related. Saurolophus, which inhabited the American West at around the same time as Parasaurolophus, was a hadrosaurine rather than a lambeosaurine hadrosaur (in plain English, it had more in common with the obscure Hadrosaurus than with the better-known

Lambeosaurus). Also, the minimally crested Prosaurolophus lived a few million years earlier. Given how many similar-looking duckbills roamed the environs of Utah seventy million years ago, do your homework before heading out into the field—or at least bring along your old "Dinosaurs: Look & Learn" View-Master.

Pentaceratops

Meaning of name: Five-horned face
Size: 20 feet long and 2–3 tons
When it lived: Late Cretaceous (75 million years ago)
Where it lived: Southwestern US
What it ate: Plants
Best viewed at: New Mexico Museum of Natural History and Science (Albuquerque)

You can learn a lot about Greek numbers by studying dinosaurs. There's no such animal (yet) as Monoceratops, but paleontologists have given us Diceratops (which may actually have been an injured Triceratops missing one if its horns), Triceratops (described on page 199), Tetraceratops (which wasn't a dinosaur at all, but a mammal-like reptile of the early Permian period), and, finally, Pentaceratops.

And here's the punch line: Pentaceratops didn't really have five horns, but rather two big horns over its eyes and a much shorter one on the end of its snout. "Horns" four and five were actually keratinous outgrowths of this dinosaur's cheekbones, and not likely to impress a hungry Bistahieversor (page 69).

The name Pentaceratops is misleading in another way: The most impressive feature of this ceratopsian isn't its horns but its enormous frill, which endows full-grown adults with skulls measuring over ten feet long (or about one-third of this dinosaur's total length). Not only does this frill make Pentaceratops an unlikely meal for a rampaging tyrannosaur, but it may serve some kind of thermodynamic function, soaking up buckets of sunshine during the day and dissipating it slowly at night. It's probably also a sexually selected characteristic (the same way male bull

elephants with bigger, more elaborate tusks get to mate with more females and thus pass on their genes).

No discussion of Pentaceratops would be complete without a mention of Titanoceratops. Announced to the world in 2011, the "titanic horned face" measures twenty-five feet from head to tail and weighs in the neighborhood of five tons, which makes it the largest ceratopsian dinosaur yet identified. The trouble is, if you viewed a Titanoceratops in the wild, you would probably assume it was an unusually large Pentaceratops—which is how the majority of paleontologists see the situation. From the perspective of seventy-five million years, it's difficult to distinguish the juvenile and elderly individuals of a given dinosaur genus from the members of a proposed new genus—the same reasoning by which another ceratopsian, Torosaurus, has long since been interpreted as an unusually long-lived Triceratops.

Platypterygius

Meaning of name: Flat flipper
Size: 23 feet long and 1–2 tons
When it lived: Early Cretaceous (145 million to 140 million years ago)
Where it lived: Oceans worldwide
What it ate: Marine animals
Best viewed at: Royal Tyrrell Museum (Drumheller, Canada)

During the Mesozoic era, marine reptiles followed a more-or-less orderly evolutionary path. First, during the Triassic period, came the semiaquatic, seal-like nothosaurs (typified by Nothosaurus). Then, in the Jurassic period, came the fully aquatic, dolphin-like ichthyosaurs (typified by Ichthyosaurus). Next, in the early Cretaceous period, were the big, vicious predators known as plesiosaurs and pliosaurs (Plesiosaurus and Pliosaurus).

And finally, during the late Cretaceous period, a big splash was made by the even more fearsome mosasaurs (you guessed it, Mosasaurus). Which brings us, in a roundabout way, to Platypterygius, which was one of the few ichthyosaurs to survive into the Cretaceous period, and so captures an important evolutionary transition in the world's oceans 145 million years ago.

For an ichthyosaur, Platypterygius was unusually sleek and streamlined, especially compared to its close relative of a few million years before, Ophthalmosaurus (page 148). Exactly how it managed to survive the Jurassic/Cretaceous boundary remains a mystery, but we do have a tantalizing clue: One Platypterygius fossil bears the undigested remains of this reptile's last meal, including birds and baby turtles.

The implication is that Platypterygius, unlike other ich-thyosaurs, had learned to expand its diet beyond fish and squids, subsisting on semiaquatic animals while the exclusively marine fauna surrounding it underwent one of its periodic shakeups. (The mass extinction at the end of the Jurassic period wasn't nearly as severe as that at the close of the preceding Triassic, or the succeeding Cretaceous, but it did have a deleterious impact on oceans worldwide.)

But enough paleoecology. What can you expect if you're swimming off the California coast and come across a school of Platypterygius? Well, you may be in for a treat. This is one of the few ichthyosaurs for which we have direct evidence of live birth. Unlike marine turtles, Platypterygius doesn't return to dry land to lay its eggs. Rather, the eggs

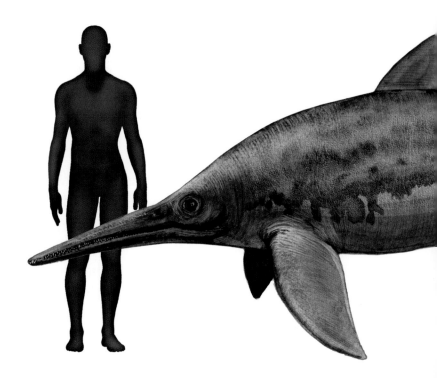

hatch inside the mother's body, whence the baby reptiles emerge hind-fin-first so as not to drown during the act of birth. (Marine reptiles aren't equipped with gills, and need to surface for air, just like whales and dolphins.)

But as cute as a baby Platypterygius can be, don't be tempted to put one in a plastic baggie and take it home for your kids, unless you want to spend the rest of your life caring for that twenty-three-foot-long, one-ton ichthyosaur in your swimming pool.

Plotosaurus

Meaning of name: Floating lizard
Size: 40 feet long and 5 tons
When it lived: Late Cretaceous (70 million to 65 million years ago)
Where it lived: Coast of western US
What it ate: Marine animals
Best viewed at: Natural History Museum of Los Angeles

Sometimes, the name bestowed on an extinct reptile doesn't quite do it justice. Plotosaurus translates from the Greek as "floating lizard," which makes it sound like the late Cretaceous equivalent of a child's inflatable pool toy. A more accurate moniker might be "gigantic, big-toothed undersea assassin that would just as soon rip your head off as give you the time of day," though one imagines the Greek genus name might be a bit unwieldy and, come to think of it, very few reptiles know how to tell time.

At forty feet long and five tons, with a sleek build, narrow jaws, and muscular flippers, Plotosaurus represented

the pinnacle of marine reptile evolution—but it still couldn't manage to escape the K/T extinction sixty-five million years ago, which consigned it to the same fate as its fellow dinosaurs and pterosaurs.

In fact, Plotosaurus may already have been on the decline. During the late Cretaceous period, sharks were rapidly gaining the edge on marine reptiles, their main advantage being that they didn't need to surface periodically for air (like all reptiles, Plotosaurus had to breathe, though possibly only once every few minutes or so). In fact, the extinction of the mosasaurs, the family of marine reptiles to which Plotosaurus belonged, flung Neptune's front door wide open for the evolution of giant sharks, culminating millions of years later in the truly stupendous Megalodon, which weighed more than fifty tons.

Postosuchus

Meaning of name: Post crocodile
Size: 15 feet long and 1,000–1,500 pounds
When it lived: Middle to late Triassic (230 million to 200 million years ago)
Where it lived: Southern US
What it ate: Small animals
Best viewed at: Texas Tech University Museum (Lubbock)

The middle Triassic period, about 230 million years ago, was a crucial juncture in reptile evolution. This was when the archosaurs, or "ruling lizards," branched off in three separate directions: One population went on to spawn the first dinosaurs; another evolved into the first pterosaurs, or flying reptiles; and a third gave rise to the first crocodiles.

The archosaurs themselves, however, never entirely disappeared, leading to confusing ecosystems in which similar-looking archosaurs, dinosaurs, and crocodiles all coexisted. Imagine a world filled with two-legged crocodiles, dinosaur-size archosaurs, and archosaur-size dinosaurs like Coelophysis (page 95), and you'll

probably be relieved that you never pursued that degree in paleontology.

This is where Postosuchus enters the picture. One of the largest predators of Triassic North America, this reptile was misidentified as a dinosaur when its remains were discovered in Texas in 1922, and then given a name ("post crocodile") that was equally deceptive, since on further examination Postosuchus turned out to be an archosaur.

Even more baffling is that no one is quite sure how Postosuchus tromped across the Texas wetlands. On the one hand this reptile possessed an elongated, crocodile-like

torso; but on the other hand, its front limbs were much shorter than its hind limbs. The (qualified) verdict is that Postosuchus was occasionally bipedal, meaning it stalked its prey on four legs but ran away on two legs when it was in danger (or perhaps reared up on its hind legs to tackle especially difficult prey).

As you may have guessed, there's still a lot we don't know about Postosuchus, so you can make a major contribution to paleontology if you happen to encounter this beast during your travels in the Lone Star State. In case Postosuchus turns out to be speedier than modern crocodiles, you don't want to tail it too closely. Also, don't be fooled by this reptile's seemingly lethargic demeanor, since this may be one of the tricks Postosuchus uses to lull its prey into a false sense of security. Whatever you do, don't go all Steve Irwin and attempt to wrestle this croc-like critter into saying "uncle"!

Prognathodon

Meaning of name: Forejaw tooth
Size: 30 feet long and 1–2 tons
When it lived: Late Cretaceous (75 million to 65 million years ago)
Where it lived: Oceans worldwide
What it ate: Mollusks
Best viewed at: Royal Tyrrell Museum (Drumheller, Canada)

As mentioned earlier in this book, the oceans of the late Cretaceous period were well stocked with mosasaurs, the sleek, vicious predators that represented the pinnacle of marine reptile evolution. Along with Plotosaurus (page 168), Prognathodon was one of the larger members of the breed, and its formidable remains have been unearthed everywhere from South Dakota to, of all places, Israel—not exactly a country known for its Mesozoic fossils. (In case you're wondering how all these Prognathodon specimens wound up in dry, landlocked regions, the earth's oceans were very differently distributed sixty-five million years ago than they are today—and much of western North America was submerged underwater!)

This explosion of mosasaur diversity—at a time when most other types of marine reptiles, including ichthyosaurs, pliosaurs, and plesiosaurs, had been rendered extinct—raises an important question: How could these finely honed killers possibly find enough undersea prey to support their growing population?

Well, a close analysis of Prognathodon's fossils provides the answer: This reptile was equipped with heavy jaws and unusually strong, thick, serrated teeth, which were ideal for chomping through the calcified shells of ammonites (a long-extinct breed of giant cephalopods), marine turtles,

and pretty much any type of animal with a crunchy exterior. In fact, one fossil specimen of Prognathodon bears direct evidence of its last meal, a turtle-and-ammonite stew supplemented with more traditional mosasaur fare, a five-foot-long prehistoric fish.

Given that you don't want to get a close-up view of its teeth, how can you tell a Prognathodon from a Plotosaurus or the dozens of other mosasaurs of the North American coast? Well, this was one of the few mosasaurs to have a two-lobed tail, similar to that of modern dolphins (as well as the ichthyosaurs that preceded it by tens of millions of years, to which Prognathodon bears a vague resemblance). By the end of the Cretaceous period, mosasaurs

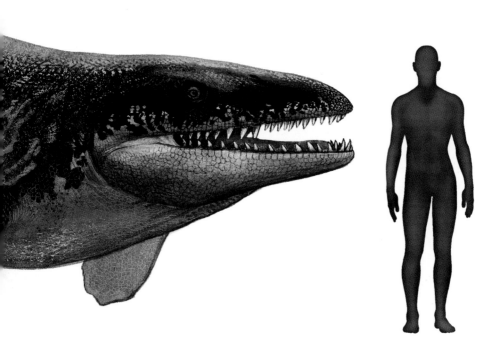

had come under increasing evolutionary pressure from sharks. The forked tail of Prognathodon made it faster and more maneuverable—meaning not only that it could out-compete sharks for prey, but it could make a quick escape when it found itself on the wrong end of the undersea food chain.

Pteranodon

Meaning of name: Toothless wing
Size: Wingspan of 20 feet and 30–40 pounds
When it lived: Late Cretaceous (85 million to 75 million years ago)
Where it lived: Western US
What it ate: Fish and small terrestrial animals
Best viewed at: American Museum of Natural History (New York)

When most people reference "pterodactyls," they're really talking about one or the other breed of flying reptile, or pterosaur: Pterodactylus, a puny, three-foot-long minnow-eater of late Jurassic Europe, or Pteranodon, a gliding, diving menace of late Cretaceous North America that attained wingspans of over twenty feet.

Americans should be proud to have Pteranodon on their side of the prehistoric ledger book. This pterosaur is represented by thousands of fossil remains, stretching from South Dakota to Alabama to Delaware, and is much better understood than the relatively enigmatic (and, did we mention, much less impressive?) Pterodactylus. Score: United States 1, European Union 0.

But forget about its size for now: Feature for feature, Pteranodon was a much more interesting creature than Pterodactylus. The most striking thing about this pterosaur was its prominent, backward-pointing head crest, which was much larger in males than in females (thanks to those thousands of fossil specimens, it's clear that this crest was a sexually differentiated feature, and not some type of "rudder" with which Pteranodon steered itself through the air). Pteranodon was also one of the few pterosaurs to completely lack teeth (hence its name, which means "toothless wing"), making it strikingly similar to the gliding seabirds

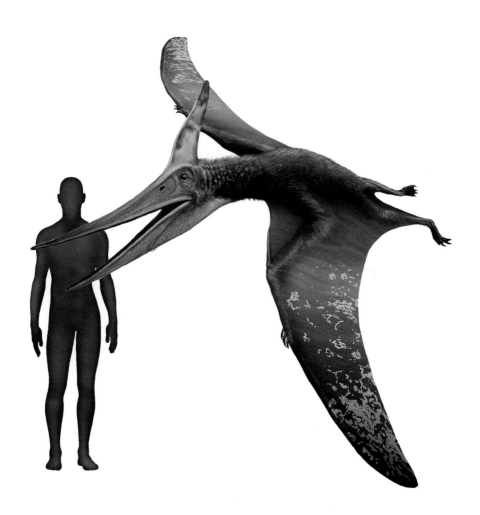

that dominated the shores of North America tens of millions of years later. (Just to be clear, birds evolved *not* from giant pterosaurs like Pteranodon but from small, feathered, flightless dino-birds like Chirostenotes; see page 90.)

At this point you might be forgiven for comparing Pteranodon to a seagull, only scaled up in size by an order of magnitude. This would be a serious mistake. Before you pack your SUV with fifty pounds of sardines and head out to the Gulf Coast, bear in mind that a flock of Pteranodons can actually be quite dangerous, especially if they all take it in mind (at the same time) to investigate the strange-looking lumps of pink, ambulatory meat that constitute you and your pterosaur-watching party. A better bet is to scout the shoreline for beached, dying whales, which the Pteranodons will descend upon so single-mindedly that you could probably approach a smaller individual and stroke its crest (that is, if you're into that kind of thing).

Quetzalcoatlus

Meaning of name: Feathered serpent god
Size: 30-foot wingspan and 200–300 pounds
When it lived: Late Cretaceous (70 million to 65 million years ago)
Where it lived: Southern US
What it ate: Fish and dinosaurs
Best viewed at: Carnegie Museum of Natural History (Pittsburgh, PA), American Museum of Natural History (New York)

They grow 'em bigger down in Texas. With its long, narrow beak and thirty-foot wingspan, Quetzalcoatlus was about the size of a small airplane, making it the largest creature of any size (including birds, reptiles, mammals, and bugs) ever to take to the sky.

But hold on a second: Did Quetzalcoatlus really fly? That's a question that has bedeviled paleontologists for the last four decades, ever since this giant pterosaur was discovered in 1971 in the Lone Star State. During the late Cretaceous period, this portion of North America was pretty much landlocked, meaning that Quetzalcoatlus couldn't have indulged in the same pelagic (ocean-flying) habit as its slightly smaller contemporary, Pteranodon (page 176).

So the possibility remains that Quetzalcoatlus spent most of its time on the ground, towering to its full, terrifying height as it stalked and ate small dinosaurs. On the other hand, if Quetzalcoatlus was indeed a flying, or at least a gliding, pterosaur, simulations have shown that it was capable of a maximum speed of eighty miles per hour and (assuming an average elevation of fifteen thousand feet) had a range of over ten thousand miles.

Clearly, this poses a dilemma for all you devoted pterosaur-watchers out there. As much as we at

FalconGuides strive for accuracy, we simply can't advise you on whether you should pack your long-range binoculars (assuming Quetzalcoatlus can fly) or an extra-big can of mace (in case this pterosaur prefers to sneak up on its prey quietly from behind).

What we can say is that, as fearsome as Quetzalcoatlus may seem in person, it's unlikely to do as much damage to your internal organs as a full-grown T. Rex, since this pterosaur only weighed about three hundred pounds—almost two orders of magnitude less than its tyrannosaur contemporary. (And by "only," bear in mind that three hundred pounds is about five times heavier than the largest flying bird alive today, the Kori Bustard of Africa—and no one in his right mind wants to tangle with a hungry Kori.)

Sauroposeidon

Meaning of name: Poseidon lizard
Size: 100 feet long and 60 tons
When it lived: Early Cretaceous (110 million years ago)
Where it lived: Western US
What it ate: Plants
Best viewed at: Oklahoma Museum of Natural History (Norman)

Every few years the popular media twists itself into a Jurassic pretzel touting the "biggest dinosaur that ever lived"—a headline usually based on an incorrect reading of a university press release or (more likely) a cynical desire to attract readers' eyeballs.

That's what happened in 1999 when the gigantic, fossilized bones of Sauroposeidon (initially mistaken for petrified trees!) were dredged out of an Oklahoma quarry. Paleontologists estimated that this sauropod measured over one hundred feet from head to tail and weighed in excess of sixty tons—impressive numbers, to be sure, but nowhere near the South American Argentinosaurus. (This scenario replayed itself in 2014 when the bones of yet another "biggest dinosaur" were unearthed in Argentina.)

Whatever its proper place in the dinosaur record books, Sauroposeidon lived at a turbulent time for giant plant-eaters, the early Cretaceous period (about 110 million years ago). Forty million years earlier, during the late Jurassic, the North American wetlands were dominated by gigantic sauropods like Brachiosaurus (page 72), Apatosaurus (page 60), and Diplodocus (page 105).

By the time Sauroposeidon appeared on the scene, these plus-size plant-eaters were on the way out, morphing over the ensuing millions of years into equally giant

titanosaurs—essentially, sauropods covered by light armor plating. Crucially, the biggest of these titanosaurs (like Argentinosaurus) lived outside North America, which after Sauroposeidon had to content itself with much smaller duckbills and ceratopsians.

But let's stop now—what with all of these qualifications, you might lose sight of the fact that Sauroposeidon was really, really big. Out in the field, it's hard to view a dinosaur in the proper perspective, so let's imagine that you encountered a full-grown Sauroposeidon in the sleepy town of Norman, Oklahoma (where a Sauroposeidon skeleton happens to be on display at the Oklahoma Museum of Natural History). The first thing you'll notice is that this dinosaur's head towers a whopping fifty or sixty feet above the ground, about the height of a six-story building—and if it happens to be taking a leisurely tour of the University of Oklahoma football stadium, you'll see that its snout pokes into the end zone whilst the end of its tail juts past the thirty-five- or forty-yard line, a field goal way out of the reach of your typical Sooner place-kicker.

Shonisaurus

Meaning of name: Shoshone mountain lizard
Size: 50 feet long and 30 tons
When it lived: Late Triassic (225 million to 200 million years ago)
Where it lived: Southwestern US
What it ate: Marine animals
Best viewed at: Nevada State Museum (Las Vegas)

In Las Vegas lingo "landing a whale" means attracting a high-roller to your casino, then (preferably) taking him to the cleaners, if you don't mind the mixed metaphor. But a Las Vegas whale has nothing on the late Triassic Shonisaurus: More than two hundred million years ago, this fifty-foot-long, thirty-ton marine reptile was the largest animal on the planet, the MGM Grand of ichthyosaurs at a time

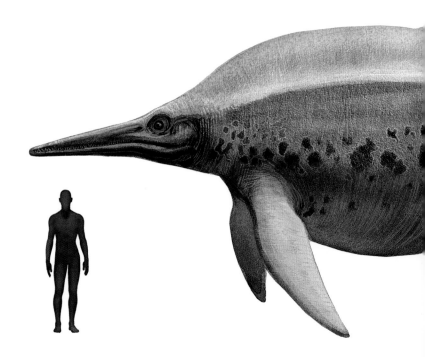

when most of its contemporaries were the equivalent of gas stations equipped with a couple of slot machines.

Discovered near the Shoshone Mountains in 1920, Shonisaurus is the official state fossil of Nevada. If you've busted your bankroll playing blackjack and need to clear your head, you can take in a specimen at the Nevada State Museum in downtown Vegas.

The question everybody asks about Shonisaurus is: What are the odds of this gigantic marine reptile landing in Nevada, of all the dusty, landlocked places on earth? As with the other ichthyosaurs, plesiosaurs, and mosasaurs discovered in the American West, the answer has to do with the distribution of the earth's oceans hundreds of millions of years ago. For much of the Mesozoic era, large portions

of Nevada (not to mention Kansas, Utah, and other now–relatively dry states) were submerged under water.

In true Vegas showman fashion, some researchers have posited the existence of a larger undersea predator, a boneless "Kraken" ancestral to modern squids and dolphins, that preyed on Shonisaurus and arranged its remains in a roughly circular fashion. The trouble is that there's absolutely no fossil evidence for this mythical beast (which didn't prevent this "theory" from generating huge headlines a few years ago).

Rumor has it that Area 51 in Nevada hosts not just the functional fragments of extraterrestrial spacecraft but also a living, breathing Shonisaurus, housed five hundred feet underground in a vast cavern filled with millions of gallons of water. (From above, of course, the installation looks just like any other bit of random desert; you have to inspect the satellite photographs closely to see the telltale seams.)

What possible interest could the US government have in Shonisaurus? Is it being weaponized for combat (a full-grown specimen can swallow an MMX warhead whole), or is it being grilled for secrets disclosed to it by ancient aliens? The answer will have to await the complete declassification of Area 51 documents, scheduled for the year 2157.

Smilodon

Meaning of name: Saber tooth
Size: 6 feet long and 500 pounds
When it lived: Pleistocene–Modern (2 million to 10,000 years ago)
Where it lived: Canada, US, and Mexico
What it ate: Meat
Best viewed at: George C. Page Museum of Natural History (Los Angeles)

Better known as the Saber-Tooth Tiger—a bit of a misnomer since it wasn't technically a tiger but an entirely different breed of big cat—Smilodon was both more and less dangerous than you might be led to believe by repeated viewings of *10,000 BC*.

To start with the good news: This Pleistocene predator had an unusually small brain (which may explain how so many Smilodons wound up mired in the La Brea Tar Pits, stalking already struggling prey), and it was much slower and more stockily built than modern cheetahs, tigers, and jaguars. Smilodon's prominent canines, which measured almost a foot long in the biggest males, weren't all they were cracked up to be, either, fracturing and shattering fairly often in the thick of paw-to-paw combat, and this big cat's jaw muscles were comparatively weak.

And now for the bad news: Pound for pound, Smilodon may have been the deadliest assassin in the history of life on earth. This cat had a habit of pouncing from the low branches of trees (of which there were many in Pleistocene North America) and digging its canines deep into the flesh of unsuspecting prey, at which point it carefully extracted its sabers, retreated to a safe distance, and waited patiently as its dinner bled to death. We don't know for sure, but there's a good chance that Smilodon hunted in packs—so

if, for instance, a wounded Titanotylopus managed to stagger away, it would perish in the presence of another Saber-Tooth Tiger, which presumably wasn't averse to enjoying its unearned meal.

Given the thousands of specimens recovered from the La Brea Tar Pits, Smilodon is particularly thick on the ground in downtown Los Angeles. If you're a native

Angeleno, you won't have to venture far to see these majestic beasts ripping into the flesh of an unwary Weimaraner—but you'll also have to share your turf with packs of ravenous predators, which can turn a task as simple as buying a gallon of soy milk into a life-and-death adventure worthy of an Ernest Hemingway novel. Your best bet for survival is if a pouncing Smilodon with your name on it happens to be distracted by a pouncing Dire Wolf (page 108)—with any luck, these two meat-eaters will collide in midair and knock each other cold.

Stegoceras

Meaning of name: Roof horn
Size: 6 feet long and 100 pounds
When it lived: Late Cretaceous (75 million years ago)
Where it lived: Western Canada and US
What it ate: Plants
Best viewed at: Royal Tyrrell Museum (Drumheller, Canada)

Not to overwhelm you with technical jargon, but during the late Cretaceous period, the plains of the western United States and Canada were dominated by two types of ornithopods: big buttheads and little buttheads.

The big butthead was Pachycephalosaurus (page 154), a fifteen-foot-long, one-thousand-pound dome-headed dinosaur whose name translates from the Greek as "thick-headed lizard." The little butthead was Stegoceras, which was only about the size and weight of your average middle-schooler and completely different in appearance from its near-homophone in the dinosaur kingdom, Stegosaurus (page 193). Stegoceras, like Pachycephalosaurus, is classified as a pachycephalosaur, the family of plant-eating dinosaurs characterized by their extra-bulbous noggins.

As with its larger relative, the most pressing question about Stegoceras is why, exactly, it evolved the three-inch-thick slab of bone comprising the top of its skull. Most paleontologists, who secretly enjoyed smashing their dinosaur figurines together as kids, hope and pray that the enlarged domes of pachycephalosaurs were used for intraspecies head-butting. This is a more dubious proposition for the half-ton Pachycephalosaurus—imagine two Hell's Angels on Harleys playing a lethal game of chicken—than it is for the much lighter Stegoceras, which may well have been

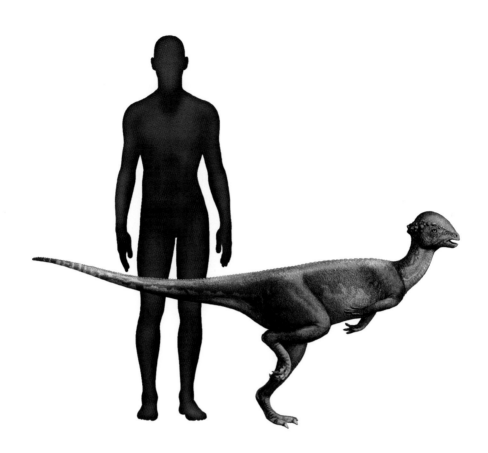

able to shake off a high-speed head butt and live to see another day.

As with Pachycephalosaurus, if Stegoceras males didn't actively butt heads, then they probably used their enlarged noggins to butt one another's flanks (as they competed for the sexual favors of females) or even the haunches of easily cowed raptors and tyrannosaurs.

Stegoceras possesses another interesting feature, which may well determine how you choose to approach this skittish beast in the wild. This dinosaur has been endowed by nature with relatively large, forward-facing eyes and stereoscopic vision, a big improvement over the splayed, cow-like peepers of its fellow hadrosaurs and ornithopods. Essentially, a herd of Stegoceras will see you coming from a mile away—and whether they decide to lower their heads and charge or flock panicked in the opposite direction will determine whether you return home to Cincinnati in a full-body cast or with a majestic piece of video footage that you can show to your friends over and over again in the safety of your man (or woman) cave.

Stegosaurus

Meaning of name: Roof lizard
Size: 20 feet long and 2–3 tons
When it lived: Late Jurassic (150 million years ago)
Where it lived: Western US
What it ate: Plants
Best viewed at: Carnegie Museum of Natural History (Pittsburgh, PA), Denver Museum of Natural History and Science

Stegosaurus is at once the most recognizable and the most poorly understood dinosaur in this book. In fact, you could write a separate book about the interpretations, reinterpretations, and misrepresentations of this late Jurassic plant-eater.

To cite just one example, it was once believed that Stegosaurus had a supplementary brain in the vicinity of its hips, since nineteenth-century paleontologists just couldn't wrap their minds around a three-ton dinosaur with a walnut-size brain. (This "brain in the butt" hypothesis, though long discredited, has persisted down to the present day: For example, in the 2013 movie *Pacific Rim*, the resident egghead posits that the Godzilla-size Kaiju have secondary brains, "just like the dinosaurs.")

The most mysterious thing about Stegosaurus, though, is the function and arrangement of its triangular plates, which are unlike anything else in the dinosaur kingdom (if you discount closely related genera like the African Kentrosaurus and the Asian Wuerhosaurus, the plates of which were differently sized and shaped).

The most likely—and the most boring—explanation is that these were a sexually selected characteristic: A male Stegosaurus with larger and more symmetrical plates had

a better chance of mating with available females. But these plates may also have helped Stegosaurus look bigger in the eyes of hungry predators (at least when they approached from the side), and they may have regulated this dinosaur's temperature, soaking up sunshine during the day and slowly radiating away excess heat at night.

To return to our original point, though, the one thing we know for sure about Stegosaurus is that it's not a very intelligent dinosaur. (As a general rule, a given animal only needs to be slightly more intelligent than its favorite food, meaning Stegosaurus was smarter than a fern.) This

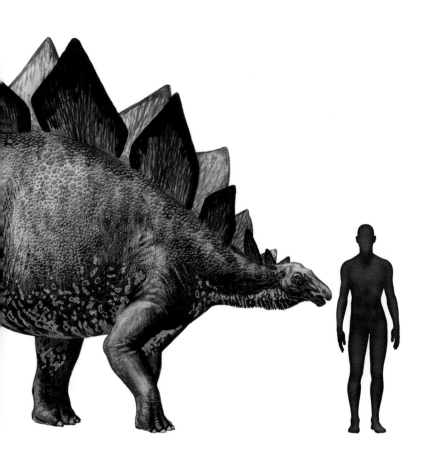

makes Stegosaurus a particularly apt choice for beginning
dinosaur-watchers, who don't want to jump into the deep
end of the Cretaceous pool by scouting out a T. Rex pack.
This plant-eater isn't very fast, so even small kids can easily
keep up with a spooked herd, and its neural apparatus is
so primitive that you could probably stroke its spiked tail
for a full five seconds before the average adult takes it in its
mind to go "moo."

Styracosaurus

Meaning of name: Spiked lizard
Size: 20 feet long and 2–3 tons
When it lived: Late Cretaceous (75 million years ago)
Where it lived: Western US and Canada
What it ate: Plants
Best viewed at: Canadian Museum of Nature (Ottawa, Canada), American Museum of Natural History (New York)

Ceratopsians—of which there are many described in this book, ranging from Agujaceratops (page 45) to Triceratops (page 199)—weren't the smartest dinosaurs on the face of the earth, which may go a long way toward explaining their characteristic horns and frills.

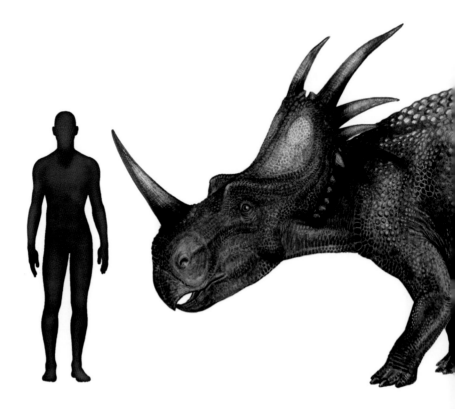

The premise runs something like this: Because these dinosaurs' apple-size brains were barely capacious enough to accommodate basic reflexes and muscle coordination, there simply wasn't any room left to pack in any cognitive functions. The varying combinations of horns and frills sported by different species were nature's way of allowing ceratopsians to recognize, and communicate with, one another, all while using a minimum of gray matter. (For example, a bright-pink frill might translate as "I am restless and feel the intense need to mate.")

If there's any truth to this theory, then Styracosaurus had an awful lot to say. The enormous frill of this ceratopsian was studded with six (or eight, depending on how you count them) horns, in addition to the two small horns

jutting out of its cheeks and the imposing two-foot-long "unihorn" on the end of its snout. Essentially, there was no mistaking Styracosaurus for any other ceratopsian, which helped maintain the cohesion of the herd (no juveniles wandering away after lunchtime and accidentally joining a group of Chasmosaurus).

Of course, the horns and frills of Styracosaurus may also have served a secondary function. One imagines that very few predators would have dared to approach this ceratopsian head-on, and it's possible that the males engaged in intraspecies combat for the right to mate with available females.

Ironically enough, the ornate head display of Styracosaurus has been of enormous selective advantage to, of all things, Styracosaurus-watchers. The Internet is rife with stories of amateur dinosaur enthusiasts who spend days ostensibly trailing a Medusaceratops (page 131), only to later realize that they were actually following a Coahuilaceratops (page 92). There's no making this mistake with Styracosaurus, although it's crucial to identify this ceratopsian on the evidence of the adults of the herd, not the babies or juveniles, whose horns and frills may not yet be fully developed.

This is a lesson that has yet to be learned by many paleontologists, who often name new ceratopsian genera without paying the requisite attention to these dinosaur's growth stages—thus, essentially, naming the same dinosaur two or three times.

Triceratops

Meaning of name: Three-horned face
Size: 30 feet long and 5 tons
When it lived: Late Cretaceous (70 million to 65 million years ago)
Where it lived: Western US
What it ate: Plants
Best viewed at: National Museum of Natural History (Washington, DC), American Museum of Natural History (New York)

For many dinosaur-watchers, the ceratopsians (horned, frilled dinosaurs) begin and end with Triceratops—never mind that dozens of genera roamed the floodplains of North America, ranging from A (Agujaceratops, page 45) to Z (the southwestern Zuniceratops). That's partly because Triceratops was the first dinosaur of its kind to vault into the national consciousness, and partly, too, because all North American ceratopsians looked pretty much alike,

except for the arrangement of their horns and frills, some of which were truly rococo in their appearance. (Asian ceratopsians, by the way, predated their more famous descendants by tens of million of years, and some of them were not only minimally horned and frilled but only the size of large dogs.)

What can we say about Triceratops, possibly the most overexposed dinosaur this side of Stegosaurus (page 193) and T. Rex (page 205)? For one thing, its name is a bit of a tease: This "three-horned face" really only had two prominent horns, one over each of its eyes, and a tiny bump on the end of its snout. For another, Triceratops progressed through various "growth stages" as it aged, which has caused paleontologists no end of trouble—individuals both young and old have been frequently misdiagnosed and assigned to their own genera. (The most famous example is Torosaurus, which may actually have been

an unusually elderly Triceratops.)

And there's no doubt this gentle plant-eater tussled occasionally with T. Rex, though it's far from a sure bet that T. Rex always emerged the winner (as a rule, predators best their prey less than half the time).

The most important thing to know about Triceratops is that this dinosaur is coveted by unscrupulous poachers, who have watched, salivating, as intact skulls sell for millions of dollars at auction—resulting in a Triceratops "black market" that international authorities have found difficult to control.

As with any dinosaur, it's strictly illegal to shoot a Triceratops in the wild, and if you witness any poaching, it's incumbent upon you to report the act to the authorities (lest you be indicted as a coconspirator). Fortunately, very few criminals can procure the hardware necessary to bag a Triceratops—forget about an elephant gun, you're gonna need a rocket launcher—and their transactions on the international arms market can easily be tracked by Interpol.

Troodon

Meaning of name: Wounding tooth
Size: 6 feet long and 150 pounds
When it lived: Late Cretaceous (70 million to 65 million years ago)
Where it lived: Western US
What it ate: Small animals
Best viewed at: Perot Museum of Nature and Science (Dallas)

Way back in 1982 the paleontologist Dale Russell wondered what might have happened if dinosaurs had escaped the K/T extinction—that is, if a meteor hadn't smashed into the Yucatán Peninsula sixty-five million years ago and wreaked a worldwide environmental catastrophe.

Russell focused his attention on Troodon, a medium-size theropod (meat-eating dinosaur) that had an unusually large "encephalization quotient," that is, a relatively large brain compared to its 150-pound body. Since Troodon was already smarter than most dinosaurs, Russell theorized that it might eventually have morphed into an anthropomorphic species—an alternative path of evolution in which intelligent humans would be replaced by intelligent reptiles.

Granted, there are a couple of problems with this scenario. First, although Troodon was certainly smarter than Stegosaurus (page 193) and Triceratops (page 199), that's not saying much considering the overall intelligence level at the end of the Cretaceous period. And second, some theropod dinosaurs did in fact evolve for millions of years after the Mesozoic era—we know them today as birds.

Although the average eagle is no doubt smarter than the average Troodon, it's still nowhere near the intelligence level of humans and only has a rudimentary (if any) grasp of tools. (Not to belabor the point, but croco-diles also survived the K/T extinction, and they were also smarter than most Cretaceous reptiles. Are intelligent crocodiles dispensing Slurpees at 7-Eleven? Not where I live.)

But let's not unfairly saddle Troodon with the speculations of a well-meaning (and widely misinterpreted) scientist. Out in the field this is a fascinating dinosaur to observe, since it partakes in a wide range of social activities: nesting, laying eggs, raising its hatchlings (at least for the first couple of weeks), and, yes, hunting mercilessly in packs. In fact, if there were any justice in the world, Troodon would have been the villain in the first *Jurassic Park* movie, rather than its slightly less intelligent contemporary Velociraptor (which was actually played by the closely related Deinonychus; see page 97 for the sad story). Such are the misguided machinations of Hollywood, at least as far as the Mesozoic era is concerned.

Tyrannosaurus Rex

Meaning of name: Tyrant lizard king
Size: 40 feet long and 7 tons
When it lived: Late Cretaceous (70 million to 65 million years ago)
Where it lived: Western US
What it ate: Other dinosaurs
Best viewed at: Carnegie Museum of Natural History (Pittsburgh, PA), American Museum of Natural History (New York)

So much has been written about Tyrannosaurus Rex—and so unrelentingly has T. Rex been glamorized in movies, on TV, and even onstage—that it's easy to lose sight of this dinosaur's obvious deficits. So in the interests of fairness, we're going to devote this page to T. Rex's shortcomings—which you may be able to witness for yourself, up close, if you're lucky (or unlucky) enough to happen upon this majestic predator out on the Utah steppes.

There's a good chance that T. Rex was feathered, like a giant chicken, at least for the first couple years of its life. We can infer this from the recent discovery of Dilong, a small Asian tyrannosaur that looked like a homicidal turkey, as well as from the profusion of small, feathered theropods from the late Cretaceous period. Granted, feathers wouldn't make T. Rex any less dangerous, but at least you could get in a healthy laugh before you were bitten in half.

Here are some other less-than-impressive characteristics:

- The arms of T. Rex were fantastically puny compared to the rest of its body, practically vestigial in relation to its massive head and well-muscled legs. (The arms weren't quite invisible; at about three feet long, they were comparable to the

arms of a full-grown human being.) No one is quite sure why this dinosaur's arms were so small; most likely they helped it clutch prey close to its chest (before delivering that killing bite) and levered it off the ground if it happened to get knocked flat.

- T. Rex had bad breath. Not just every-day, forgetting-to-brush-your-teeth bad breath, but epic bad breath, the kind of bad breath that sets small birds aflame from fifty feet away. Because

there's no evidence that T. Rex ever flossed, this dinosaur always had rotting chunks of flesh wedged between its teeth, which aided in the delivery of "septic bites" (that is, if Rex didn't happen to bite its prey in half on the first try, the unfortunate animal would die a few days later from a massive bacterial infection).

- T. Rex wasn't necessarily the apex predator of the late Cretaceous period. This so-called "tyrant lizard king" may have spent most of its day scavenging already-dead corpses, only actively hunting when it faced starvation. (To be fair, though, no theropod worth its back teeth would willingly overlook an already-dead corpse—so if T. Rex was a coward, so was every meat-eating dinosaur of the Mesozoic era.)

Just a few things to keep in mind as you observe your first T. Rex out in the field. Hold your breath, stay out of arm's length, and don't attempt to play dead (as you would with a grizzly bear), and you stand a fifty-fifty chance of returning home to Dubuque alive. OK, maybe thirty-seventy, but we don't want to discourage you.

Utahraptor

Meaning of name: Utah thief
Size: 23 feet long and 1,000 pounds
When it lived: Early Cretaceous (125 million years ago)
Where it lived: Western US
What it ate: Other dinosaurs
Best viewed at: Natural History Museum of Utah (Salt Lake City)

Tiny progenitors tend to give rise, after tens of millions of years, to much larger descendants. Witness the first toddler-size dinosaurs of the Triassic period or the doglike mammals that lay at the root of the whale evolutionary tree.

Sometimes, though, this process works in reverse, which explains how Utahraptor—by far the largest raptor that ever lived—existed fifty million years before the more famous, and much smaller, Deinonychus (page 97) and Velociraptor. Whereas the early Cretaceous Utahraptor tipped the scales at half a ton, its descendants of the late Cretaceous period weighed a couple of hundred pounds, max, and most were the size of chickens. (Utahraptor's slashing hind claws were almost a foot long, which made the curved cuticles of Deinonychus look like baby scissors!)

Why did raptors diminish in size toward the end of the Mesozoic era? The most likely explanation is that they faced increasing competition from tyrannosaurs like Albertosaurus (page 48) and T. Rex (page 205), which evolved "right side up" from their small, feathered forebears of the late Jurassic period and hogged all the plus-size prey.

Utahraptor, by contrast, was one of the apex predators of its early Cretaceous ecosystem, and may have hunted in packs to bring down giant, three-ton ornithopods like

Iguanodon. (By the way, while we have no direct evidence that Utahraptor was covered with feathers, this seems like a reasonable inference to make given the discovery of so many feathered raptors—and the likelihood that even T. Rex hatchlings looked like monstrous chickadees.)

So dangerous is Utahraptor—and so stark the consequences if a restless pack should follow unwary dinosaur-watchers back to civilization—that the state of Utah has issued strict regulations about how closely you can approach this raptor, and even what you can bring with

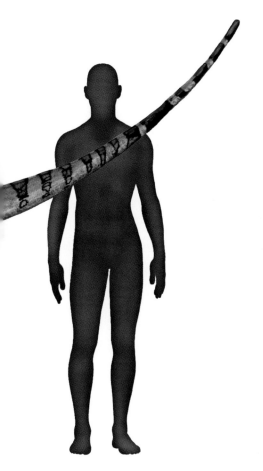

you on your expedition. You'll have no choice but to set up camp at least a mile or two away (be sure to pack your long-range binoculars) and stay within your SUV at all times, as these curious dinosaurs have been known to be attracted by campfires, the glow of smartphone screens, and even spirited conversation.

Come to think of it, why don't you just stay home and leave the Utahraptor-monitoring to the professionals, who can simply buzz this killer from a distance in government-surplus black helicopters?

Woolly Mammoth

Size: 12 feet long and 5–7 tons
When it lived: Pliocene–Modern (5 million to 10,000 years ago)
Where it lived: US, Mexico, and Canada
What it ate: Plants
Best viewed at: Royal BC Museum (Victoria, Canada), American Museum of Natural History (New York)

Of all the prehistoric animals in this book, the Woolly Mammoth is the only one that you may really be able to see in your lifetime—not stuffed and behind glass in a natural history museum but actually roaming the western plains. The reason is that the last Woolly Mammoths only went extinct an eyeblink ago, geologically speaking, and a fair number of them have been preserved in the permafrost of northern Canada and the Eurasian steppes.

It may yet be possible to recover fragments of intact DNA from these quick-frozen individuals, combine them with the DNA of modern elephants, and clone something very close in appearance and behavior to a living, breathing Woolly Mammoth, a process that's been given the headline-friendly tag "de-extinction."

But just because we may (emphasis on the "may") be able to clone a Woolly Mammoth, does that mean we should? There's a good case to be made that *Mammuthus primigenius* went extinct for a reason: It was big (up to seven tons) and needed correspondingly large amounts of vegetation to sustain its lifestyle. Also, the Woolly Mammoth was vulnerable to predation by that most dangerous of all mammals, ancestral humans, who coveted it for its meat and for its shaggy fur (which could provide winter coats for an entire tribe). We can't even protect endangered African elephants from poachers, so why should we have better luck protecting an entire herd of Woolly Mammoths, the ivory of which would be all that much more valuable?

This scenario doesn't only apply to the Woolly Mammoth, though it's certainly the most viable candidate for de-extinction—other prospective species that have been laid on the table include the recently extinct Dire Wolf (page 108) and Saber-Tooth Tiger (page 187). (As for the

dinosaurs discussed in this book, you can lay your hopes and fears to rest—the only place they'll ever be cloned is Jurassic Park, because there's no hope of recovering their intact DNA.)

Will your children, or your children's children, one day be able to hop in the family hovercraft and visit Pleistocene Park, a fully stocked ecosystem, complete with monorail and snack bar, somewhere in the vicinity of Utah? Don't bet against it, but don't go reserving your tickets just yet.

About the Author

Bob Strauss is the author of two best-selling question-and-answer books that range across the expanse of science, biology, history, and culture: *The Big Book of What, How, and Why* (2005) and *Who Knew?: Hundreds & Hundreds of Questions & Answers for Curious Minds* (2007). Over the past two decades, he has written and edited for various scientific, medical, and general-interest publications, including *Entertainment Weekly*, *Family Circle*, and *ConsumerSearch*. For the past ten years, he has been the dinosaur expert at About.com (dinosaurs.about.com).

About the Illustrator

Ukrainian illustrator Sergey Krasovskiy describes himself as a paleoartist. Since his childhood, he has had a love of paleontology and, especially, of dinosaurs. Growing up in Donbass, a region of Ukraine famous for its coal mines—which produced huge amounts of slag and rock—Krasovskiy collected excavated fossils of ancient ferns. In other layers of rock there have been found shark teeth and the remains of mosasaurs, huge carnivorous aquatic lizards.

Krasovskiy studied art at the Lugansk Art College and, thanks to the Internet, has acquired an international reputation as a freelance illustrator of Paleolithic creatures.

He work will soon appear in two Russian publications: an encyclopedia called the *Great Illustrated Atlas* of the *Dinos* *e Past of* *the Ea* escribes *as an* work *of Rus* Roman Evsee

Be and his famil arkov. He de